BRAVE BOYS

BIBLE TRIVIA

50 ADVENTUROUS QUIZZES

Conover Swofford

SHILOH kidz
An Imprint of Barbour Publishing, Inc.

ISBN 978-1-64352-647-8

Published by Shiloh Kidz, an imprint of Barbour Publishing, Inc., 1810 Barbour Drive, Uhrichsville, Ohio 44683, www.shilohkidz.com

Our mission is to inspire the world with the life-changing message of the Bible.

Member of the
Evangelical Christian
Publishers Association

Printed in the United States of America.

000486 0920 BP

CONTENTS

Guys, you can change the world
for good. . .when you become
the person God wants you to be.

This brand-new Bible trivia challenge is based on the popular picture book *100 Adventurous Stories for Brave Boys*. It's a fun way to help you learn the scriptures to make yourself and your world better!

Test your knowledge of what the Bible says, and along the way you'll learn a lot about 50 key character traits, including:

- Ambition
- Calling
- Faithfulness
- Self-Denial
- Thankfulness
- Zeal
- and many more

These fun quizzes will show you what God wants for your life—and the lives of the people around you. As a bonus, each quiz also includes a short story about a real man who changed history for good. . .for God!

Note: Answers immediately follow each quiz.

QUIZ 1

AMBITION

(a strong dream, goal, or desire)

His name was Dwight Lyman Moody, but he went by D. L.

He sold shoes for his uncle. He couldn't find another job. He felt worthless. Even after he came to know Jesus, D. L. struggled. He wanted to be useful to God, but he didn't always make good choices. . .and he had trouble reading. He started a Sunday school class for children, but those who visited said he had trouble sounding out hard words in the Bible, and often skipped over them. But D. L. Moody became a world-traveling preacher who started a church, three schools, and a publishing company.

And God knows what you can become too. His love changed a simple shoe salesman into someone who published books and preached sermons that influenced millions for Jesus.

God can make *your* dreams come true if you let Him. In the quiz that follows, some of these people let God's love lead them. . .and some didn't.

1. Nadab and Abihu, the sons of Aaron, wanted to be priests in their own way rather than God's way. When they offered "strange" fire, the kind God had not told them to use, He sent what to destroy them?

a. fire
b. water
c. an earthquake
d. a snake

2. When a rich young man asked Jesus what he could do to inherit eternal life, Jesus told that man that he should give all his money to the poor. The rich young man

a. did what Jesus told him
b. ran away and got married
c. went away sad
d. laughed at Jesus

3. Jacob wasn't the firstborn, but he still wanted his brother Esau's special firstborn blessing. How did Jacob trick his blind father, Isaac, into giving him Esau's blessing?

a. Jacob dressed like Esau
b. Jacob served his father a special meal
c. Jacob had his mother, Rebekah, help him
d. all the above

4. When the prophet Samuel anointed Saul king of Israel, Saul

a. said, "Who? Me?"

b. tried to hide

c. yelled, "Yippee!"

d. refused the crown

5. King David's son Absalom wanted to be king instead of his father. So Absalom started a secret campaign to

a. kill the captain of David's army

b. marry David's wives

c. make all the people like him better than David

d. chase his brothers out of the country

6. James and John, two of Jesus' disciples, had their mother ask Jesus to give them important places in His kingdom. The other disciples

a. thought that was a great idea

b. got angry with them

c. asked Jesus for the same favor

d. quit being Jesus' disciples

7. Nimrod was a mighty hunter who didn't worship God. Nimrod built a famous city that Jonah would later preach in. That city was

a. Nineveh

b. Jerusalem

c. Cairo

d. New York

☆ ANSWERS ☆

1. a (Leviticus 10:1-2 KJV)

2. c (Mark 10:17-22)

3. d (Genesis 27:13-19)

4. b (1 Samuel 10:20-22)

5. c (2 Samuel 15:6)

6. b (Matthew 20:20-24)

7. a (Genesis 10:8-11)

QUIZ 2

ATTITUDE

(the way you think or feel about something or someone)

Jonah was a prophet commanded to share God's message. But Jonah paid to get on a boat sailing *away from* the city he was supposed to deliver the message to. He didn't want to deliver God's words, so he ran. Big mistake.

God sent a fish big enough to swallow Jonah when he was tossed into the sea by the ship's crew. For three days, Jonah lived (and prayed!) inside the fish. He had time to think, and he changed his mind and attitude.

The people of Nineveh were mean, rude, and angry. Jonah would have been happy to see God punish them. He thought they deserved it. But God loves to show mercy. When Jonah delivered God's message, the people stopped being rude, mean, and angry. That was when Jonah *started* doing what the people of Nineveh had just *stopped* doing.

We should always be happy when God works a miracle in the lives of people He loves (and He loves everyone). Thankfulness is a great way to make sure you have a positive attitude every day. In the quiz that follows, see what kind of attitudes these people had.

1. In order for Jesus to come to earth to save us from our sins, He had to
a. humble Himself
b. become like a servant
c. look like a man
d. all the above

2. When Mary sat at Jesus' feet, just listening to Him, Jesus told her sister Martha that Mary's attitude was good. According to Jesus, Mary
a. was lazy
b. had chosen what was most important
c. should be yelled at
d. would go help Martha

3. Jesus told a parable about a judge who was mean to a woman. Jesus said the judge was mean because
a. he didn't fear God
b. he just liked being mean
c. he was born that way
d. other people were mean to him

4. Ahab was the nastiest king Israel ever had. The Bible says that no one before Ahab did more _____ in the eyes of the Lord.
a. stupid stuff
b. damage
c. sin and evil
d. destruction

5. Jesus once called James and John the "Sons of Thunder," apparently because they were angry. That was when they asked Jesus if they could call down fire on a village that

    a. laughed at them
    b. wouldn't welcome Jesus
    c. kept an idol in the town square
    d. smelled like old fish

6. Jesus told a parable about a Pharisee and a tax collector who went to the temple to pray. The Pharisee was proud and selfish and prayed about

    a. himself
    b. the tax collector
    c. the Jews
    d. his dog

7. In the same parable, the tax collector worshipped God and prayed

    a. loudly
    b. that God would pity him
    c. for his wife
    d. for the Pharisee

☆ ANSWERS ☆

1. d (Philippians 2:7–8)

2. b (Luke 10:42)

3. a (Luke 18:1–8)

4. c (1 Kings 16:30)

5. b (Luke 9:51–56. Of course, Jesus wouldn't let them do it!)

6. a (Luke 18:11)

7. b (Luke 18:13)

QUIZ 3

BELIEF

(the trust you have in a person, thing, or idea)

If you ever doubt yourself, thinking you'll never amount to much, think of Billy Sunday.

Billy came from a poor family, and his dad died just a few weeks after he was born. Mom tried to make a good life for her family, but after a while she had to send Billy to an orphanage. There Billy discovered baseball, and he eventually got a chance to play in the major leagues! He played eight seasons with three different teams.

But Billy had doubts about himself. Once in Chicago, he heard a small band playing a hymn his mother had sung when he was young. It wasn't long before Billy became a Christian. . . and he moved from playing baseball to preaching God's Good News.

For years Billy traveled the United States, preaching to all who would listen. It's been said that more than a *million* people came to know Jesus because he shared God's love. But even with so many good things happening, Billy still needed his wife, Nell, to help him and cheer him on.

Sometimes it's hard to believe God loves and accepts us. But the Bible is clear that He does—that's why He sent Jesus to die for our sins! In the following quiz, see what you know about the belief that trusts in God's goodness.

1. God promised Abraham that he would have a son and his descendants would one day live in the "Promised Land." What did God say Abraham's belief counted as?
   a. total success
   b. victory
   c. being right with God
   d. solid gold

2. When the Israelites saw the miracles that Moses and Aaron did, the Israelites believed
   a. that God was troubled about them
   b. that God had seen their misery
   c. that Aaron had spoken the truth
   d. all the above

3. Jesus asked two blind men if they believed He could heal them. They said, "Yes, Sir!" and Jesus
   a. walked away
   b. healed them
   c. laughed
   d. told them to see the priest

4. The New Testament believers came together to worship and fellowship and they
   a. believed in the apostles' teachings
   b. spent time together daily
   c. shared all their possessions
   d. all the above

5. God so loved the world that He gave His one and only Son that whoever believes in Him
a. shall not perish
b. shall have eternal life
c. shall get rich
d. a and b

6. The Israelites wandered in the wilderness for forty years because they didn't believe God would give them the Promised Land. Why didn't they believe what God had said?
a. they were afraid of the people who already lived in the land
b. they hated Moses
c. Aaron told them lies about God
d. they were distracted by grasshoppers

7. The Bible says that anyone who comes to God must believe that
a. God exists
b. God is nice
c. God wants to punish them
d. God knows everything

☆ ANSWERS ☆

1. c (Genesis 15:6)

2. d (Exodus 4:29-31)

3. b (Matthew 9:27-29)

4. d (Acts 2:42-47)

5. d (John 3:16)

6. a (Numbers 13:31)

7. a (Hebrews 11:6)

QUIZ 4

CALLING

(a strong desire to a certain way of life or job)

Some people seem to be born to do great things. What if you were born to tell other people how wonderful someone *else* was? Would you ask for a new project?

John the Baptist was given that kind of job—*before* he was even born. In fact, the prophet Isaiah talked about John's job (almost seven hundred years earlier), when he wrote, "Make the way ready for the Lord in the desert. Make the road in the desert straight for our God" (Isaiah 40:3).

When John started getting things ready, people came out to hear him preach and see what he would do. But when Jesus arrived, John knew what his job was: he talked about Jesus, saying, "He must become more important. I must become less important" (John 3:30).

Is it hard to be happy for people when they seem more important than you? When God gave John the job of preparing the world for Jesus, he was happy that God's greatest message was finally being heard. God had given John a perfect calling.

In the following quizzes, let's see what you know about the callings of other Bible characters.

1. Before he was born, an angel told John the Baptist's father that his son had a calling from God to
   a. get people ready for the Lord
   b. sing and dance
   c. write important books
   d. yell at the people

2. Jesus called Peter and Andrew to be His disciples while they were
   a. hunting
   b. cooking
   c. eating
   d. fishing

3. Out of the twelve tribes of Israel, which tribe was called to be priests?
   a. Levi
   b. Joseph
   c. Gad
   d. Zebulon

4. The book of 2 Peter says that Christians are to make our calling sure so that we will never
   a. fear
   b. fall
   c. cheat
   d. sin

5. God called Moses to lead the children of Israel out of Egypt. God got Moses' attention by showing him
a. a singing sheep
b. a burning bush
c. a glowing cloud
d. a towering mountain

6. When God first called Abraham, He asked Abraham to
a. become a farmer
b. marry Ruth
c. tend God's sheep
d. move to another country

7. God called to the prophet Samuel in the night while Samuel was
a. reading
b. eating
c. lying down
d. praying

☆ ANSWERS ☆

1. a (Luke 1:17)

2. d (Matthew 4:18-20)

3. a (Exodus 38:21)

4. b (2 Peter 1:10)

5. b (Exodus 3:2)

6. d (Genesis 12:1)

7. c (1 Samuel 3:3-4)

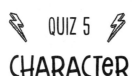

QUIZ 5

CHARACTER

(being good; doing the right thing)

It seems unfair to be punished for doing the right thing. Maybe you know what that's like.

You know what got Daniel into trouble? Praying! King Darius was tricked into signing a stupid law that made Daniel's morning-noon-and-night prayers to God illegal. But Daniel knew it was right to pray, so he prayed just as he'd always done.

That's when he was taken to the king, who "tried to think of a way to save Daniel" (Daniel 6:14). But the tricksters reminded the king that he couldn't go back on his word. He sadly sent Daniel to the lions' den.

The good news is that God saved Daniel, by sending an angel to keep him safe. That law that seemed so unfair ended up reminding everyone that God is amazing. King Darius said, "He is the living God and He lives forever. His nation will never be destroyed and His rule will last forever. He saves and brings men out of danger, and shows His great power in heaven and on earth. And He has saved Daniel from the power of the lions" (Daniel 6:26–27).

Daniel showed good character. Other Bible people had both good and bad character. What do you remember about the kind of character God wants you to have?

1. Who did King Darius's law say everyone needed to pray to?

a. King Darius
b. idols
c. a statue
d. themselves

2. Jesus said that to enter the kingdom of heaven you must become like little

a. ants
b. children
c. monsters
d. men

3. According to the Proverbs, the woman of noble character will have children who do what?

a. honor her
b. live long lives
c. clean their rooms
d. send her flowers

4. Although David knew that he would someday be king, how did he respond when King Saul tried to kill him?

a. David refused to try to kill King Saul
b. David ignored King Saul
c. David didn't believe King Saul was trying to kill him
d. David took a long ocean cruise

5. Barnabas—who sold a field and gave the money to help poor Christians—was nicknamed
   a. Son of Generosity
   b. Son of Comfort
   c. Son of Silver
   d. Sonny

6. Elisha's servant, Gehazi, showed bad character by lying to Naaman to get silver and valuable robes. What was Gehazi's punishment?
   a. he was beaten
   b. he was put in prison
   c. he got Naaman's bad skin disease
   d. he was severely scolded

7. Samson was strong in body but weak in character. What did he let Delilah do that made his strength disappear?
   a. kiss him
   b. hold his hand
   c. cut his hair
   d. cook him broccoli

☆ ANSWERS ☆

1. a (Daniel 6:7-9)

2. b (Matthew 18:3)

3. a (Proverbs 31:28)

4. a (1 Samuel 24:10)

5. b (Acts 4:36-37)

6. c (2 Kings 5:26-27)

7. c (Judges 16:18-19)

QUIZ 6

CHEERFULNESS

(being happy)

Patrick Henry Hughes was born without eyes. He can't walk. He's never seen a sunset or felt the sand between his toes on a beach.

But when he was just nine months old, he began to play the piano. In high school, he played trumpet in the marching band—his dad pushed his wheelchair. Patrick Henry is a recording artist and an author, and he loves Jesus.

Patrick Henry could have gotten mad, but he had a different way of thinking: "I see blindness more as an ability and sight more as a disability, because there are some people with sight who tend to judge others by what they see on the outside, but I don't see that. I don't see the skin color, the hair style, or the clothing people wear; I only see that which is within a person."

Everything you think is bad is an important part of your story—and maybe it's the right story to cheer up someone else when they're having a bad day. Maybe Patrick Henry's story cheers you up too.

God can accomplish a lot in you if you have a cheerful attitude. See if you can remember about what the Bible says about cheerfulness.

1. The Bible tells us to give to God cheerfully because He _____ a cheerful giver.
a. blesses
b. loves
c. empowers
d. throws a party for

2. The Proverbs say that a glad heart makes your _____happy.
a. body
b. friends
c. face
d. parents

3. The Proverbs also say a glad heart is as good for your body as
a. behaving in school
b. winning a race
c. talking to your friends
d. taking medicine

4. When Jesus walked on the water, He called out to His disciples, "Be of good cheer. It is I. Do not. . .
a. jump out of the boat."
b. scream."
c. be afraid."
d. doubt My abilities."

5. Why did Jesus say every Christian should "be of good cheer"?
   a. "I have overcome the world."
   b. "You are going to heaven."
   c. "God owns the cattle on a thousand hills."
   d. "There will never be another great flood."

6. According to the book of Ecclesiastes, when should people be most cheerful?
   a. when they're young
   b. when they're middle aged
   c. when they're old
   d. when they're dead

7. According to the Psalms, when you make yourself happy in the Lord, what do you get?
   a. chocolate ice cream
   b. money and health
   c. unending sunshine
   d. the desires of your heart

☆ ANSWERS ☆

1. b (2 Corinthians 9:7 KJV)

2. c (Proverbs 15:13)

3. d (Proverbs 17:22)

4. c (Mark 6:50 KJV)

5. a (John 16:33 KJV)

6. a (Ecclesiastes 11:9)

7. d (Psalm 37:4)

QUIZ 7

COMPASSION

(loving-kindness)

James W.C. Pennington was born a slave and given as a gift to a slaveholder. That doesn't seem fair—but it was the way things were done in the early 1800s. James eventually escaped and got the opportunity to attend Yale University after being taught to read and write. He became a preacher, and people liked to hear him speak.

James knew slavery was wrong. He helped raise money to send some slaves back to Africa because they wanted to go home. He loved his freedom, but he often felt as if he would one day be captured and sent back to slavery again. James was free in New York, but he knew that God would make him free forever through Jesus. And he believed that God would be honored if His compassion was offered to every single person.

Compassion is a kind of love, the desire to help other people when they're in trouble. What do you recall of these compassionate people in the Bible?

1. Who showed compassion to a widow named Ruth by letting her glean (pick up the leftovers) in his field?

a. Boaz
b. Jesus
c. Paul
d. Peter

2. In Jesus' story of a stranger who took compassion on a man who had been robbed and beaten up, Jesus said this good stranger was a

a. Jew
b. Ninevite
c. Samaritan
d. Russian

3. When a lame beggar asked Peter and John for money, how did Peter show the man compassion?

a. He gave him a drink of water
b. He healed him so he could walk
c. He patted him gently on the head
d. He gave him two dollars

4. Jesus had compassion on two sisters by raising their brother, Lazarus, from the dead. Who were the sisters?

a. Rachel and Leah
b. Jezebel and Athaliah
c. Anna and Huldah
d. Mary and Martha

5. The Bible says that God shows His compassion to people
a. every morning
b. when the sun is shining
c. only on Sundays
d. every third Christmas

6. When two blind men asked Jesus to have compassion on them, Jesus
a. gave them money
b. healed them so they could see
c. sent them to the temple
d. told them to come back in a week

7. When Jesus showed compassion on a demon-possessed man, He sent the demons into a herd of
a. pigs
b. deer
c. cows
d. cats

☆ ANSWERS ☆

1. a (Ruth 2:8-9)

2. c (Luke 10:33)

3. b (Acts 3:7-8)

4. d (John 11:1)

5. a (Lamentations 3:23)

6. b (Matthew 9:27-30)

7. a (Mark 5:1-13)

QUIZ 8

COURAGE

(bravery)

Young David, who would one day be king of Israel, spent most of his time guarding sheep. His brothers, who served in Israel's army, seemed angry when David visited them, then asked questions about the nearly nine-feet-tall enemy Goliath. That giant had challenged any soldier from Israel's army to fight him. If the soldier won, the enemy's army would serve Israel. If the soldier lost, Israel would serve the enemy's army. But no one had the courage to take up Goliath's challenge . . .except for David.

King Saul tried to help the shepherd boy get ready to fight. But the king's armor was too big. David, knowing God was bigger than any giant, chose to trust the Lord to help him fight Goliath.

With five stones and a slingshot, David faced Goliath, saying, "You come to me with a sword and spears. But I come to you in the name of the Lord. . . . For the battle is the Lord's" (1 Samuel 17:45, 47).

Knowing God was with him, David made his slingshot whistle. One of his stones flew through the air and knocked Goliath down. The shepherd boy had defeated the "giant" who'd threatened God's sheep.

When you need courage, ask God. He will help you battle your giants. Let's see if you know how God gave courage to other people.

1. The Jewish priests put Peter and John in jail for preaching about Jesus. When Peter and John got out of jail

    a. they told the priests nothing could stop them from preaching

    b. they ran away and hid

    c. they left Jerusalem

    d. none of the above

2. When Joshua sent two spies into Jericho, Rahab hid the spies from the king because

    a. she hated the king

    b. she believed in God's power

    c. Joshua told her to

    d. the spies made her

3. When Daniel was told that he could only pray to King Darius, Daniel

    a. prayed only to King Darius

    b. didn't pray at all

    c. continued to pray to God three times a day

    d. hid under his bed

4. Anyone trying to see the king without his invitation could be put to death. But Esther knew that to save her people, she had to try. When Esther went to see the king

    a. his bodyguards stopped her

    b. he made her leave the kingdom

    c. he had her put to death

    d. he held out his scepter

5. After Elijah ran away from the wicked Queen Jezebel, God gave Elijah the courage to
a. apologize to her
b. shoot her with an arrow
c. go back the way he'd come
d. be a spy in her palace

6. Because Stephen, an early Christian, told the Jews about Jesus, the Jews
a. accepted Jesus
b. stoned Stephen to death
c. ignored him
d. put him in jail

7. Even though Paul knew he would be arrested if he went to Jerusalem to preach about Jesus, Paul
a. went anyway
b. hid
c. ran away
d. went sailing

☆ ANSWERS ☆

1. a (Acts 4:19-20)

2. b (Joshua 2:11)

3. c (Daniel 6:10)

4. d (Esther 5:2)

5. c (1 Kings 19:15-19)

6. b (Acts 7:59)

7. a (Acts 21:10-17)

QUIZ 9

CURIOSITY

(wanting to know something)

Nobody likes bad news, especially if it's about himself. Bad news can sound like losing a job, car, or home, or like an injury, accident, or disease. That's what bad news sounded like to teenager Corey Montgomery.

The doctor told him he had sickle cell anemia. Corey didn't know what that was, but he learned that it would cost thousands of dollars to treat, and many African Americans get the disease. He was African American. All that added up to bad news.

Corey didn't tell anyone what the doctor said. He wanted to act as normal as possible. When assigned a science project, Corey chose sickle cell anemia as his topic. He learned being tired and having pain was normal. He also learned his heart and lungs could be damaged. More bad news.

Yet then Corey found there was a possible cure using a bone marrow transplant. He researched how to find someone whose bone marrow was like his—and it saved his life! It's not often a school assignment saves a life, but that's Corey's story—and it was trust that helped Corey. He didn't just trust there was a cure. He trusted that God loved him.

Corey used his curiosity to learn about his disease and help others. What can you learn from the curiosity of these Bible people?

1. It was the serpent's tempting and Eve's curiosity about the tree of _____ that made her disobey what God told her and eat fruit from that tree.
    a. learning about good and evil
    b. the knowledge of love
    c. sugar Cain
    d. apples

2. Moses was tending to a flock of sheep when a curious sight caught his eye. Moses saw
    a. his brother, Aaron
    b. another flock of sheep
    c. a burning bush
    d. a glowing angel

3. When Jesus talked about water to the Samaritan woman at the well, she was curious to know
    a. how Jesus could get water from the well
    b. how the water Jesus spoke of would keep someone from becoming thirsty again
    c. if Jesus was the One called the Christ
    d. all the above

4. Jesus told the story of the Good Samaritan because someone asked Jesus
    a. What's good about a Samaritan?
    b. How can I be saved?
    c. Who is my neighbor?
    d. Where are you going?

5. Simon the Sorcerer saw believers in Jesus receiving the Holy Spirit after Peter and John laid their hands on them. Simon thought it was a magic trick and tried to get Peter and John to

a. stop doing it
b. go away
c. sing and dance
d. sell it to him

6. When some men of Bethshemesh looked into the Ark of the Covenant when they weren't supposed to, God

a. struck them dead
b. gave them leprosy
c. blessed them
d. turned them into a pillar of salt

7. When an earthquake opened the prison doors for Paul and Silas, the jailer asked them

a. Is this your fault?
b. Is everyone alive?
c. What must I do to be saved?
d. Do you want a lawyer?

☆ ANSWERS ☆

1. a (Genesis 2:17)

2. c (Exodus 3:1–3)

3. d (John 4:11–26)

4. c (Luke 10:29)

5. d (Acts 8:18)

6. a (1 Samuel 6:19. God had already warned the people very strongly against doing this.)

7. c (Acts 16:30)

DeDICATION

(being faithful or devoted to something)

Giving up is easy. Dropping out is natural. Showing up and holding on are harder. God never gives up—and neither should you.

Robert Moffat was a missionary in southern Africa. He often looked at the skies beyond his village and wondered about the people he couldn't see. Robert always thought there just wasn't enough time to reach all the people he knew lived beyond his village. Maybe that's why he said, "We shall have all eternity in which to celebrate our victories, but we have only one swift hour before the sunset in which to win them."

Robert dedicated his life to reaching people in Africa for Jesus. Robert never gave up on them. And he inspired other people to do the same.

Have you ever given up on something that seemed too hard? Ask God to help you be brave and to keep trying, no matter what.

What can you learn from these biblical examples of dedication to God?

1. Solomon made a sacrifice of 22,000 cattle and 120,000 sheep when he dedicated
   a. his palace
   b. a new bridge
   c. the house of the Lord
   d. his first son

2. Who told Samson's parents before Samson was born that he was to be a Nazirite, a person dedicated to the Lord?
   a. Samson's grandparents
   b. a talking donkey
   c. a prophet
   d. an angel

3. When Mary and Joseph took the baby Jesus to the temple to dedicate Him to the Lord, they had to
   a. offer a sacrifice
   b. pay taxes
   c. hide Jesus from the Roman soldiers
   d. tell their parents

4. Joshua was the dedicated follower of Moses. After Moses died, God made Joshua
   a. the leader of Israel
   b. wear Moses' coat
   c. go to Egypt
   d. carry Moses' bones

5. When Abraham arrived in the land God had led him to, he dedicated that land to God by building _____ to the Lord.

   a. a tower
   b. a temple
   c. an altar
   d. a statue

6. Esther risked her life by going uninvited to see the king because she was dedicated to

   a. keeping her good looks
   b. saving her people
   c. being queen
   d. killing Mordecai

7. In order to stay with Naomi, Ruth dedicated herself to Naomi, Naomi's people, and Naomi's

   a. health
   b. boyfriend
   c. well-being
   d. God

☆ ANSWERS ☆

1. c (1 Kings 8:62–63)

2. d (Judges 13:2–5)

3. a (Luke 2:22–24)

4. a (Joshua 1:1–2)

5. c (Genesis 12:8)

6. b (Esther 4:13–16)

7. d (Ruth 1:16)

⚡ QUIZ 11 ⚡

DILIGENCE

(careful and continual effort)

God wants you to do something for Him, to be involved in His plan. Even though you might help others, pray for someone, or show kindness, God wants something more.

Charles Finney was a preacher. The one thing he wanted to do for God was tell people about His Son, Jesus. Charles felt like he was wasting time if someone's future didn't change because of the Good News he shared.

Charles believed in 2 Timothy 4:2: "Preach the Word of God. Preach it when it is easy and people want to listen and when it is hard and people do not want to listen. Preach it all the time. Use the Word of God to show people they are wrong. Use the Word of God to help them do right."

And that's just what Charles did. He told people that no matter what they thought, God was *always* right. Charles wanted his life to be filled with moments when he could share what he believed. He didn't want anyone to think you could say nice things about Jesus but never obey what He said.

Like Charles, spend your time wisely. Share Jesus. Show others the way He's changing you.

Now you can meet some people who knew how to "do" diligence.

1. Jesus went about doing good because
   a. God anointed Him with the Holy Spirit
   b. God was with Him
   c. Jesus was setting a good example
   d. all the above

2. The book of Proverbs says that lazy hands make a man poor, but diligent (or steady or hardworking) hands bring
   a. warts
   b. wealth
   c. anger
   d. friendship

3. When the children of Israel returned from captivity, they had to rebuild the city of Jerusalem. Ezra told them to be especially diligent to rebuild
   a. their houses
   b. their barns
   c. the temple—God's house
   d. their playgrounds

4. The apostle Paul was diligent about preaching the Gospel of Jesus. Even when he was in prison in Rome, he preached to
   a. his mom
   b. everyone who visited
   c. the emperor
   d. the garbage collector

5. Because the prophet Jeremiah was diligent to tell the Israelites God's message, the king of Judah
a. threw Jeremiah into prison
b. told him to stop talking or die
c. finally listened
d. a and b

6. When Laban tricked Jacob by giving him Leah as his wife, Jacob diligently worked for Laban another seven years so he could have Leah's sister, _____, as his wife too.
a. Ruth
b. Naomi
c. Rachel
d. Esther

7. When Samuel came to anoint David to be king of Israel, David was diligently tending to his father's
a. sheep
b. goats
c. vineyards
d. horses

☆ ANSWERS ☆

1. d (Acts 10:38; John 1:1; 13:15)

2. b (Proverbs 10:4)

3. c (Ezra 7:23)

4. b (Acts 28:30-31)

5. d (Jeremiah 37:18; 38:24)

6. c (Genesis 29:26-28)

7. a (1 Samuel 16:11-13)

QUIZ 12

DUTY

(things a person should or must do)

Elisha was the student of the prophet Elijah. He didn't mind doing small jobs. If Elijah needed water, Elisha got it for him. If he needed someone to carry something, Elisha carried it. If Elijah needed company, Elisha walked and talked with him.

God was preparing Elisha to do bigger things. Soon people turned to Elisha for help. They knew this prophet served God and that God helped him.

The people had stopped following God. But as Elisha began teaching them, they began following God again. It was easy to believe God was with Elisha. God did miracles through him. He made poisonous water safe, fed more than a hundred men with a few loaves of bread, healed a Syrian soldier with a skin infection, and raised a child from the dead.

Elisha was willing to do what God asked, and he helped teach four different kings over fifty years. Elisha's life is a good example of what is written in 1 Peter 4:10: "God has given each of you a gift. Use it to help each other."

God can use you too. Start obeying and trusting God in small things. Then, when He has bigger plans, you'll be ready to take on even bigger duties!

Now let's check out how other people did with their God-given duties!

1. Hezekiah was one of the best kings Judah ever had. When Hezekiah became king, the people of Judah were worshipping false gods. So Hezekiah did his duty and
    a. repaired the temple
    b. celebrated Passover
    c. tore down all the places where false gods were worshipped
    d. all the above

2. Before he became a Christian, Saul (who later became Paul) thought he was doing his duty to God by
    a. hurting the church
    b. shaving his head
    c. burning Bibles
    d. giving up wine

3. Because he was the nearest relative by law, it was Boaz's duty to marry
    a. Mary
    b. Ruth
    c. Martha
    d. Naomi

4. God gave Jonah the duty of preaching to the city of Nineveh but Jonah
    a. ran away
    b. pretended he didn't hear God
    c. locked himself in his bedroom
    d. asked a friend to go instead

5. Jesus dutifully came to earth and died on the cross
  a. to save us from our sins
  b. because He loves us
  c. in obedience to His Father
  d. all the above

6. In Acts there are several mentions of a man named Barnabas who helped the disciples by
  a. selling a field and bringing them the money
  b. bringing Paul to them
  c. going on a missionary journey with Paul
  d. all the above

7. When Joseph, the husband of Mary, found out that Mary was expecting a child, he
  a. broke up with her
  b. married her
  c. married her sister
  d. ran away

☆ ANSWERS ☆

1. d (2 Chronicles 29–31)

2. a (Acts 8:3. Obviously, Saul was mistaken!)

3. b (Ruth 4:1–10)

4. a (Jonah 1:2–3)

5. d (Matthew 1:21; Romans 5:8; Matthew 26:39)

6. d (Acts 4:37; 9:27; 13:2–4)

7. b (Matthew 1:18–24)

⚡ QUIZ 13 ⚡

ENDURANCE

(sticking with something no matter what)

David Brainerd had dreams. But his parents died and he became an orphan when he was only nine years old. He wanted a college education. But he was sent home from school when he became sick. He wanted to be a missionary. But if he was to be a missionary he would have to work while he was sick.

David coughed a lot, but despite his serious illness, he worked with several Indian tribes in New York and New Jersey. He traveled more than three thousand miles by horse as a missionary. He preached, started a new school, and translated the Psalms for the people he worked with.

David didn't let anything—being orphaned, kicked out of school, or sick—stop him from following his dream. David had endurance. That means he *stuck to* his dream no matter what. He said, "We should always. . .glorify God, and do all the good we possibly can."

For three years, David worked as a missionary. He wrote a journal that's been read by many. His story has encouraged men, women, and children to become missionaries. David died before his thirtieth birthday. But he followed his dream because his dream looked a lot like God's plan.

It takes endurance to stick to what you know is right. Let's see what endurance you have while taking this quiz.

1. When the Israelites fought the Amalekites, as long as Moses raised his hands to God, the Israelites won. But when Moses got tired and had to lower his hands, the Amalekites won. So when Moses had trouble holding up his hands

    a. Aaron and Hur held them up for him

    b. the Amalekites claimed total victory

    c. Moses passed out

    d. he got a frozen shoulder

2. The book of Hebrews says we are to run with endurance the race God has marked out for us. That race is a symbol for

    a. how we live our Christian lives

    b. the Olympics

    c. preaching

    d. raising a family

3. When Paul and Silas were beaten and thrown into prison in Philippi, they endured their hardship by

    a. telling jokes

    b. thinking good thoughts

    c. praying and singing hymns to God

    d. making friends with other prisoners

4. The psalm writer says he can endure the valley of the shadow of death because

    a. he's not afraid of anything

    b. God is with him

    c. he has friends

    d. he's heading for the mountain of light

5. Jesus endured all the horror of being crucified on the cross

    a. for the joy of being with God later

    b. because He loves us

    c. because He's the only one who could save us from our sins

    d. all the above

6. Although King Saul hunted David and tried to kill him, David endured it and didn't try to harm King Saul in any way because

    a. King Saul was the Lord's chosen king

    b. David was afraid of King Saul

    c. King Saul was David's master

    d. Saul would later become the Christian Paul

7. Deborah, the only female judge of Israel, was told by God to command Barak to go fight the Canaanites. But Barak couldn't endure the idea and said he would only go if

    a. his mom could come with him

    b. Deborah went with him

    c. he could wear the king's armor

    d. he heard the command directly from God

☆ ANSWERS ☆

1. a (Exodus 17:8–13)

2. a (Hebrews 12:1)

3. c (Acts 16:25)

4. b (Psalm 23:4)

5. d (Hebrews 12:2; Romans 5:8;
   Acts 4:12)

6. a (1 Samuel 24:6)

7. b (Judges 4:8)

QUIZ 14:

FAITHFULNESS

(loyalty to something or someone)

Have you ever sensed God asking you to do something that was really, really hard? Maybe you just didn't want to do it. Maybe it seemed scary.

Abraham was already old when God told him to move to a place he'd never even visited. God told Abraham, "Leave your country, your family and your father's house, and go to the land that I will show you. And I will make you a great nation. I will bring good to you" (Genesis 12:1–2). And because God asked, Abraham did the hard thing. He moved. And when Abraham got to the land of Canaan, God told him, "I will give this land to your children and to your children's children" (Genesis 12:7).

God's promises may seem to take a long time to be fulfilled, but you can be sure that when God makes a promise, He will keep it. Abraham had to wait twenty-five years for the baby boy God had promised him. He named him Isaac.

God wants you to be faithful, just as He is faithful to you. Check out these examples of people who were faithful to God, and people to whom God was faithful.

1. Cornelius was faithful to God even though he was not Jewish. Cornelius was
   a. a Roman "centurion," or army captain
   b. the king of another nation
   c. a Roman tax collector
   d. a slave in Pilate's household

2. The book of Romans says that faith comes from
   a. praying every day
   b. hearing the Gospel message
   c. telling others about Jesus
   d. obeying your parents

3. Baby Moses' parents showed their faith by
   a. praying in public
   b. holding worship services at their house
   c. not fearing Pharaoh's threat to kill Hebrew babies
   d. telling their friends about God

4. What city did God say Joshua would defeat if he faithfully marched around it for seven days?
   a. Jerusalem
   b. Nineveh
   c. Bethlehem
   d. Jericho

5. Because Solomon had faith in God, he asked God for
   a. love
   b. wisdom
   c. money
   d. a wife

6. What did faithful Ruth tell her widowed mother-in-law, Naomi, as Naomi planned to return to Jerusalem?
   a. "I will go where you go"
   b. "I will live where you live"
   c. "Your God will be my God"
   d. all the above

7. Faithful Deborah believed God when He said He would give Israel victory over their enemy Sisera. Because Israel's commander Barak did not, Deborah told him,
   a. "The Lord will sell Sisera into the hands of a woman."
   b. "Your chariot will get stuck in the mud."
   c. "Oh you of little faith. Why do you not believe?"
   d. "Just do it! And God will reward you."

☆ ANSWERS ☆

1. a (Acts 10:1)

2. b (Romans 10:17)

3. c (Hebrews 11:23)

4. d (Hebrews 11:30)

5. b (1 Kings 3:9–12)

6. d (Ruth 1:16)

7. a (Judges 4:9)

QUIZ 15

FRIENDSHIP

(being a buddy)

It's very good to have a friend who really cares about you. Before David was the king of Israel, he had just that kind of friend. Jonathan was supposed to be king after his father, Saul, died. But God had different plans. David was anointed by the prophet Samuel to be the next king. Instead of becoming jealous of the shepherd boy, Jonathan became David's best friend.

David would come to play music for King Saul. Afterward, David would spend time with Jonathan. Saul didn't want Jonathan to be friends with David, but when Jonathan grew up, David remained his best friend.

One day David heard King Saul wanted to kill him. David asked Jonathan to warn him if this was true. Jonathan learned that Saul was angry enough to kill David.

Jonathan was sad when he told David the news: "Go in peace. For we have promised each other in the name of the Lord, saying, 'The Lord will be between me and you, and between my children and your children forever.' Then David got up and left, and Jonathan went into the city" (1 Samuel 20:42).

Jonathan was a true and courageous friend. He thought friendship was more important than becoming king.

Let's see what more the Bible can teach us about friendship!

1. How does the Bible say Jonathan loved David?
   a. as he loved himself
   b. as high as the heavens are above the earth
   c. as deep as the ocean
   d. as much as he loved video games

2. Who were Jesus' closest friends among the twelve disciples?
   a. Judas, Judas Iscariot, and Simon the Canaanite
   b. Peter, James, and John
   c. Philip, Bartholomew, and Thomas
   d. Andrew, Matthew, and James, the son of Alphaeus

3. According to the Proverbs, when does a friend love you?
   a. only in good weather
   b. when he agrees with you
   c. all the time
   d. every third Sunday

4. When Judas betrayed Jesus with a kiss, Jesus said, "Friend. . .
   a. watch your step"
   b. do what you came to do"
   c. are you sure you want to do this?"
   d. get your lips off me"

5. Abraham was called the friend of
   a. Jesus
   b. Judas
   c. Lot
   d. God

6. What did the three friends Shadrach, Meshach, and Abednego do to get themselves thrown into a fiery furnace?
   a. write on the bathroom wall
   b. refuse to bow before a golden statue
   c. forget the king's birthday
   d. preach to the Ninevites

7. Some people tried to disrespect Jesus by saying He was not only a friend of sinners but also of
   a. drunks
   b. overeaters
   c. tax collectors
   d. all of the above

☆ ANSWERS ☆

1. a (1 Samuel 18:3)

2. b (Matthew 17:1; Mark 14:33;
   Luke 9:28)

3. c (Proverbs 17:17)

4. b (Matthew 26:50)

5. d (James 2:23)

6. b (Daniel 3)

7. d (Matthew 11:19)

⚡ QUIZ 16 ⚡

GENEROSITY

(showing you're ready and willing to give)

How do you fit the whole story about Jesus on one page? Simple: you can't. But here's a really, really short history of His life:

Jesus was born in Bethlehem in a stable. His first visitors were shepherds. When He was twelve years old, He stayed behind in Jerusalem to talk with the religious leaders. By the time He was thirty, He began telling people that God loved *everyone*, not just a few. He showed them that God was more interested in their hearts than their good deeds. That He could heal and perform miracles. That He cared about people.

Jesus said He would die to pay for the sins of every person who has ever lived. One Friday, long ago, He died on a cross—but by Sunday, He had risen from the dead! Now He offers eternal life when you simply accept His gift of forgiveness and rescue. We call the story of Jesus "Good News." Because it's the best news you could ever read.

Even though you can't out give Jesus, He wants you to show His generosity to others. What more can you learn about generosity in this quiz?

1. When a rich young man asked Jesus what he must do to inherit eternal life, what did Jesus tell him?
   a. sell everything and give the money to the poor
   b. buy your parents a nice house
   c. sponsor a missionary
   d. build a church

2. After the tax collector Zaccheus met Jesus, how much of his money did he promise to give to the poor?
   a. all of it
   b. one tenth
   c. half of it
   d. not a penny

3. When a lame beggar asked Peter and John for money, Peter told him, "I have something better I can give you in the name of Jesus Christ." Then Peter
   a. handed him a Bible
   b. smiled warmly
   c. took him by the hand, helped him up, and healed him
   d. gave him new crutches

4. When God showed Abraham's servant that Rebekah was the one who would be Isaac's wife, Abraham's servant gave Rebekah and her family
   a. a homemade pizza, extra cheese
   b. silver, gold, and precious gifts
   c. whatever they asked for
   d. blessings from Abraham

5. What did Jesus use to generously feed five thousand men (plus women and children) who'd come out to hear Him teach?

    a. a food truck
    b. five loaves and two fishes
    c. the cattle on a thousand hills
    d. quail and manna

6. When the Queen of Sheba visited King Solomon, she brought him much gold and spices. In return, King Solomon gave her

    a. half his kingdom
    b. many servants
    c. lots of olive oil
    d. whatever she asked for

7. What did Dorcas make and give to the poor people of her city of Joppa?

    a. clay pots
    b. clothing
    c. medicine
    d. glazed doughnuts

☆ ANSWERS ☆

1. a (Mark 10:21)

2. c (Luke 19:8)

3. c (Acts 3:1–8)

4. b (Genesis 24:53)

5. b (Matthew 14:17–21)

6. d (1 Kings 10:13)

7. b (Acts 9:39)

QUIZ 17

GOOD DEEDS

(doing things helpful to others)

Have you ever heard of Albie Pearson? He was a baseball player who retired more than fifty years ago.

Albie was short. Hardly any of his teammates thought he could help their team win. He was offered a pair of shoes, a suitcase, and $225 a month if he could do well enough to stay on the team. He was supposed to be a pitcher, but Albie became an excellent hitter. He even won the Rookie of the Year award! Then Albie hurt his back and made the difficult choice to hang up his cleats. He had played for the Washington Senators, the Baltimore Orioles, and the Los Angeles Angels.

After baseball, Albie's faith led him to become a pastor. He preached. He built orphanages in Ecuador and Zambia. He helped those who needed help. At an age when most people choose to retire, Albie and his family started a ranch to take care of orphan boys. Albie explained that anyone can follow God: "He's just looking for a bunch of people to love Him and be an example in loving others."

Why not think of some good deeds *you* can do? Maybe you'll get some ideas as you solve this do-gooders' quiz!

1. Dorcas helped the poor by sewing clothes for them. When she died, the people she had helped begged Peter to do something. So,
    a. he handed out Kleenex
    b. he prayed, then raised Dorcas from the dead
    c. he learned how to sew
    d. he organized a clothing drive

2. The Pharisees used trumpets to announce their good deeds so that people would admire them. Jesus said
    a. God would not reward the Pharisees for that
    b. kazoos should be used instead of trumpets
    c. they were good men
    d. you should do that too

3. Jesus told a parable about a man who did a very good deed by taking care of another man who had been robbed and beaten. That parable is called
    a. The Lost Sheep
    b. Lazarus and the Rich Man
    c. The Pearl of Great Price
    d. The Good Samaritan

4. When Joseph was in prison in Egypt, he helped Pharaoh's cupbearer and baker by
    a. teaching them Hebrew
    b. interpreting their dreams
    c. telling the guards to go easy on them
    d. getting them jobs in the prison kitchen

5. When Naaman found out he had leprosy, his wife's maid did a good deed and told Naaman's wife that he should
   a. go see the prophet Elisha for a cure
   b. visit the king's nurse
   c. wash in the Pool of Siloam
   d. try some calamine lotion

6. What does the book of James say our good deeds prove?
   a. our wisdom
   b. our education
   c. our faith in God
   d. all the above

7. Jesus said that you should let your light shine before men so they could see your good deeds and
   a. do the same
   b. bless you
   c. honor your Father in heaven
   d. not stumble in the darkness

☆ ANSWERS ☆

1. b (Acts 9:39–41)

2. a (Matthew 6:2–4)

3. d (Luke 10:25–37)

4. b (Genesis 40:8)

5. a (2 Kings 5:1–3)

6. c (James 2:14)

7. c (Matthew 5:16)

QUIZ 18

GROWING UP

(becoming older and wiser)

John Newton said, "I am not what I ought to be, I am not what I want to be, I am not what I hope to be. . .but still I am not what I used to be." This is his story.

John was a preacher and a hymn writer. But his life was filled with sad events and bad choices. John's mom died when he was seventeen. A year later he was forced to serve in the British navy. He tried running away but was caught.

It wasn't long before John worked on a ship that brought slaves from Africa. A storm near Ireland almost sunk the ship. John knew something needed to change. *He called out to God for help.*

John read the Bible, grew in faith, and wrote the hymn "Amazing Grace." But he needed to know God more. So God continued to work on and teach John.

What John used to be was nothing he was proud of. *What he hoped to be* was something to look forward to. *What he wanted to be* meant he hadn't given up on himself. *What he ought to be* meant John had learned the difference between right and wrong.

Kids—and grownups—are learning from God all the time. Let's look at how some youngsters grew up in God.

1. This boy's mother, Hannah, dedicated him to the Lord—so he grew up in the temple with the priest, Eli.
   a. Samuel
   b. Samson
   c. Saul
   d. Solomon

2. How old was Jesus when His parents lost Him in Jerusalem and found Him in the temple talking with the religious teachers?
   a. 3
   b. 5
   c. 7
   d. 12

3. The Bible says that Jesus grew strong in mind and body and in favor with God and
   a. parents
   b. men
   c. cousins
   d. friends

4. Why did God tell the prophet Samuel to choose young David to be the next king instead of an older brother?
   a. "he has the biggest muscles"
   b. "this man is my chosen instrument to proclaim my name to the Gentiles"
   c. "he is without blame, a man who is right and good"
   d. "man looks at the outside of a person, but the Lord looks at the heart"

5. What Old Testament prophet questioned his calling by telling God, "I am only a boy"?
a. Jeremiah
b. Obadiah
c. Moses
d. Habakkuk

6. How did God respond to the boy-prophet of question 5?
a. "Before you were born, I set you apart as holy"
b. "Do not be afraid. . .for I am with you"
c. "I have chosen you this day"
d. all the above

7. The youngest king of Judah was seven years old when he took the throne. His name was
a. Jesus
b. Saul
c. Joash
d. Jonathan

☆ ANSWERS ☆

1. a (1 Samuel 1:20, 24–28)

2. d (Luke 2:42)

3. b (Luke 2:52)

4. d (1 Samuel 16:7)

5. a (Jeremiah 1:6)

6. d (Jeremiah 1:4–10)

7. c (2 Chronicles 22:10–23:11)

QUIZ 19

HELPING

(giving someone a hand)

William Booth was not a typical preacher. He had a low growl in his voice and a very long beard. William faced many struggles that might have caused him to give up, but with each new challenge he believed God had something bigger for him. William said, "Work as if everything depended upon work, and pray as if everything depended upon prayer."

When William Booth was young, his family became poor. He had to leave school and begin working at age thirteen. Two years later, William was training himself to become a preacher. His friend said the story of God's great rescue by sending Jesus to save humans was the greatest story anyone could share.

Each new ministry William worked with helped him learn what he needed to begin the Salvation Army. This ministry worked to make things easier for people who struggle. When people knew the Salvation Army cared about them, they listened more carefully to the message the Salvation Army shared.

People needed help, but they needed Jesus even more. William said, "If I thought I could win one more soul to the Lord by walking on my head and playing the tambourine with my toes, I'd learn how!"

What special talents can you use to help others? Let's see if these quiz questions might give you any ideas!

1. Baby Moses' mother, Jochebed, sent the boy's sister to watch over him while he floated on a river in a basket. Moses' sister was named
    a. Maureen
    b. Eve
    c. Miriam
    d. Ruth

2. Who helped Daniel get back out of the lions' den?
    a. his mother, who raised him
    b. his father, who taught him
    c. his friends, who loved him
    d. the king, who put him there

3. When King Saul was upset, David played soothing music for him on what instrument?
    a. tambourine
    b. harp
    c. trumpet
    d. electric guitar

4. The apostle Paul said Jesus had taught that we are happiest
    a. when we give rather than receive
    b. after we have worked hard for others
    c. falling asleep while praying for people
    d. if we build churches in foreign lands

5. Which of Jesus' disciples brought his brother, Peter, to meet Jesus?
a. Andrew
b. James
c. John
d. Paul

6. God told Elijah to hide from wicked King Ahab. Then God helped Elijah by sending ravens to bring him
a. sticks for a fire
b. manna and bananas
c. bread and meat
d. macaroni and cheese

7. The Golden Rule says you are to help other people by doing for them
a. whatever they ask
b. what Jesus has done for you
c. what others have done for you
d. what you would like them to do for you

☆ ANSWERS ☆

1. c (Exodus 2:3–4; Numbers 26:59)

2. d (Daniel 6:23)

3. b (1 Samuel 16:23)

4. a (Acts 20:35)

5. a (John 1:40–41)

6. c (1 Kings 17:6)

7. d (Matthew 7:12)

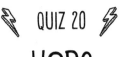

QUIZ 20

HOPE

(believing good things will happen as God promised)

Robert Preston Taylor was a chaplain. That means he was a pastor for soldiers. He was a member of the United States Air Force and helped soldiers with their faith.

Robert served during World War II and was taken prisoner when American forces surrendered to the Japanese. He walked in what was called the Bataan Death March, as Japanese soldiers moved more than fifty thousand American soldiers to a camp for prisoners of war. Many died.

The Japanese allowed Robert to continue sharing God's love with soldiers, and he ministered to thousands of men in the hospital. But then Robert was kept in a cell alone for trying to get food and medicine to soldiers in the hospital. He spent fourteen weeks away from those who needed him.

Robert spent more than three years as a prisoner of war. But he never pushed God away even when it would have been easy to give up. Robert said, "In the prison camp you live one day at a time but with your eye on the future. . .with. . .hope and faith."

When hard times come, trust God to give you hope and strength—no matter what happens.

Now it's time for a quiz about hope. *Hope* you do well!

1. What did the apostle Paul tell Titus was the Christian's "great (or blessed) hope"?
   a. healthy and wealth
   b. world peace
   c. the second coming of Jesus
   d. a happy family

2. The prophet Jeremiah said that God has plans for His people, plans to give them hope and a
   a. blessing
   b. past
   c. sign
   d. future

3. The apostle Paul said hope is one of three things that will last when everything else is gone. The other two things are:
   a. faith and love
   b. worry and doubt
   c. soul and spirit
   d. fire and water

4. Hannah was glad God gave her the son she had hoped for. When he was born she named him
   a. Samuel
   b. Samson
   c. Shadrach
   d. Sennacherib

5. The Bible says faith is being sure of what you hope for and
   a. what you once had
   b. what you are told
   c. what you can't see
   d. what you have

6. When the children of Israel were slaves in Egypt, they hoped for someone to save them. Who did God send?
   a. Pharaoh
   b. Joshua
   c. Adam
   d. Moses

7. How does the book of Hebrews describe our Christian hope?
   a. as food for the soul
   b. as oxygen for the soul
   c. as peace for the soul
   d. as an anchor for the soul

☆ ANSWERS ☆

1. c (Titus 2:13)

2. d (Jeremiah 29:11)

3. a (1 Corinthians 13:13)

4. a (1 Samuel 1:19–20)

5. c (Hebrews 11:1)

6. d (Exodus 3:11)

7. d (Hebrews 6:19)

QUIZ 21

HOSPITALITY

(friendly and kind treatment of guests or strangers)

Jesus wants you to be kind, but to whom? Jesus knew you would want to know, so He told the story of the Good Samaritan.

A man walked alone between Jerusalem and Jericho. Along the road were lots of hiding places for robbers. Some robbers jumped the man, beat him up, took his belongings, and ran. The man was hurt so badly he couldn't walk. He couldn't even call for help.

Two people came by. They noticed the man was hurt. They should have helped him but didn't. Both men worked in the temple.

Just when the injured man thought there was no hope, a Samaritan came by. Everybody was unfriendly to Samaritans. How could the beaten man expect someone considered an enemy to offer help? But the Samaritan stopped and took care of him. This Good Samaritan showed hospitality by taking the man to an inn and paying the innkeeper to watch over him.

Jesus wants everyone to understand that sometimes help comes from places and through people you would never expect. Probably the biggest lesson Jesus wanted you to know is that *you* can be brave enough to help someone even when other people won't. Helping someone is showing true hospitality. Maybe the quiz that follows will give you some ideas of how you can help others, just like Jesus does.

1. The book of Hebrews says that when you are hospitable to strangers sometimes you are actually entertaining _____ without knowing it.

  a. celebrities
  b. escaped prisoners
  c. superheroes
  d. angels

2. Jesus often stayed at the home of Lazarus and Lazarus's two sisters

  a. Ruth and Naomi
  b. Rachel and Leah
  c. Mary and Martha
  d. Jezebel and Athaliah

3. When Solomon was king, he showed hospitality by having the Queen of Sheba for a visit. Why did she come?

  a. she had heard of Solomon's fame
  b. she wanted to borrow some money
  c. she was visiting all the rulers in the Middle East
  d. she took a wrong turn on the highway

4. When a Pharisee named Simon hosted Jesus, the Lord corrected Simon because

  a. the food ran out
  b. the host was upset by a woman who washed Jesus' feet
  c. the house was dirty
  d. all the above

5. Which church leaders are supposed to be especially good at hospitality?
   a. music directors
   b. Sunday school teachers
   c. pastors and elders
   d. curriculum writers

6. When three men sent by God visited Abraham, he immediately
   a. gave them a drink of water
   b. told Sarah to bake bread for them
   c. made them an offering
   d. offered them his tent

7. To help uncover a plot against her people, Esther used hospitality and invited the king and the wicked man named _____ to a banquet.
   a. Saul
   b. Ahab
   c. Haman
   d. Judas

☆ ANSWERS ☆

1. d (Hebrews 13:2)

2. c (John 11:1-3)

3. a (2 Chronicles 9:1)

4. b (Luke 7:36-50)

5. c (Titus 1:5-9)

6. b (Genesis 18:1-7)

7. c (Esther 5:4)

INFLUENCE

(using power to convince someone for good)

Hudson Taylor started China Inland Mission. More than eight hundred missionaries came to China because of Hudson's example. He spent more than fifty years working there.

George Müller, who ran several orphanages in London, influenced Hudson. He told Hudson to pray for God's help before asking anyone else for help. Writer and preacher Charles Spurgeon encouraged Hudson never to give up. Missionary Jim Elliot, preacher Billy Graham, and evangelist Luis Palau were all influenced by the life and ministry of Hudson Taylor.

Other people can influence your choices. At the same time, your choices can influence even more people.

Hudson Taylor changed the way people thought of missionary work when he said, "God uses men who are weak. . .enough to lean on Him." Lean hard. God is always strong enough.

How might Hudson's words influence you? How might you influence others? Who influences you? Check out how influence affected the lives of people in the following quiz questions.

1. Influence can be good or bad. Only one queen of Israel and one queen of Judah are mentioned by name in the Bible and they happen to be wicked and mother and daughter. Their names are

    a. Jezebel and Athaliah

    b. Ruth and Naomi

    c. Mary and Martha

    d. Leah and Dinah

2. Paul told Timothy that Timothy's faith was strong because of Lois and Eunice who were Timothy's

    a. two older sisters

    b. grandmother and mother

    c. church deacons

    d. Sunday school teachers

3. Jesus was a very good influence on people because He went about doing good and teaching people about the kingdom of God. Jesus did what He did because

    a. He was doing what His Father God taught Him

    b. He was doing what Moses told Him to do

    c. He wanted fame and fortune

    d. He wanted the disciples to like Him

4. When Peter preached his first sermon on the day of Pentecost and told all the people how Jesus had come just like the scriptures said He would

    a. the people called Peter a liar

    b. the apostles applauded

    c. about 3,000 people were saved and baptized

    d. the high priest threw Peter in jail

5. Paul called Titus "my true son in the faith" because
   a. Titus was Paul's son
   b. it was Paul who taught Titus to believe in Jesus
   c. Titus was Jewish, like Jesus
   d. Titus had married Paul's daughter

6. The Lord said Ahaziah was a wicked king because Ahaziah chose to walk in the wicked ways of his grandfather
   a. King Ahab
   b. King Absalom
   c. King Saul
   d. King Hezekiah

7. What did John the Baptist call Jesus, causing two of his disciples to follow the Lord?
   a. the Creator of Heaven and Earth
   b. the Voice of One in the Wilderness
   c. the Power from On High
   d. the Lamb of God

☆ ANSWERS ☆

1. a (1 Kings 19:1–2; 2 Kings 9:30; 11:1)

2. b (2 Timothy 1:5)

3. a (John 8:28)

4. c (Acts 2:41)

5. b (Titus 1:4)

6. a (2 Kings 8:27)

7. d (John 1:35–37)

QUIZ 23

JOY

(a feeling of great happiness or delight)

Jonathan Edwards spent a lot of time outside. He explored the height of trees, the depth of creeks, and the width of canyons. You might think he was just a boy who loved being outdoors, but Jonathan came to think of everything God made as a way to show His creativity, awesomeness, and wisdom.

Jonathan was very interested in spiders, the effects of light, and how God made vision so people could see all of God's big and small creations.

The things Jonathan saw convinced him to say, "I will live for God. If no one else does, I still will." Jonathan followed God for the rest of his life. He was a preacher, he wrote books, and he was the president of a college, but God's wonder always found him applauding God for His creation.

When you're sitting in science class, taking a walk, playing in the park, counting the night stars, or just looking out your window, remember that God is a master Creator, and He is happy when you enjoy what He made. That's what Jonathan Edwards did!

God's Word, the Good News about Jesus, and the God of hope fill people with joy. Check out the next quiz to see what else the Bible teaches about joy.

1. Psalm 100 says, "Call out with joy to the Lord, all
_____."
   a. the earth
   b. you people
   c. you shepherds
   d. of nature

2. God loves you so much that He has much joy in you
and rejoices over you with
   a. gladness
   b. singing
   c. love
   d. angels

3. Jesus said that there is more joy in heaven over one
sinner who is sorry for his sins than over ninety-nine
people who
   a. are right with God
   b. are happy in their sins
   c. go to church every Sunday
   d. have never heard of Jesus

4. How old was John the Baptist when he first felt joy
by learning about his relative, Jesus the Son of God?
   a. 2 years
   b. 6 years
   c. 20 years
   d. he was still in his mother's belly

5. Whose weeping was turned to joy when Jesus showed up alive near His empty tomb?
   a. the apostle John
   b. Mary Magdalene
   c. Martha
   d. Pontius Pilate

6. The Bible says that weeping and sadness may remain for a night but joy
   a. never comes on time
   b. comes with the new day
   c. remains for two nights
   d. has a way of finding you

7. What event caused David to dance with joy before the Lord?
   a. his victory over Goliath
   b. the birth of his son Solomon
   c. his marriage to Saul's daughter Michal
   d. the arrival of the ark of the covenant in his capital city

☆ ANSWERS ☆

1. a (Psalm 100:1)

2. b (Zephaniah 3:17)

3. a (Luke 15:7)

4. d (Luke 1:41)

5. b (John 20:15–18)

6. b (Psalm 30:5)

7. d (2 Samuel 6:16)

QUIZ 24

KEEPING PROMISES

(doing what you say you'll do)

Many years passed between the time God said He would send a huge flood on the world and the time Noah let the animals onto the ark. Most people didn't do what God told them to do, but Noah and his family obeyed and were promised safety on that big boat.

It took many, many years for Noah to build the ark. We can imagine that lots of people laughed at him for building a boat so far from a lake or ocean. But because Noah was a friend of God, he was brave enough to do what God asked—even when no one thought it made sense. When the rain began to fall, Noah remembered all of God's promises were true. He knew God's plans were amazing. He could trust God to protect him and his family.

The rain beat against the ark for forty days and nights. Noah's family cared for the animals. When the time was right, every person and animal left the ark. They were safe. God had done it—He kept His promise!

God always keeps His promises, and we should keep ours too. Take this quiz to see how much you remember of the Bible's word on promises.

1. God promised Noah that God would never again flood the earth. The sign that God would keep that promise was

    a. a rainbow in the sky

    b. a cloud shaped like an umbrella

    c. a dove with an olive leaf in her beak

    d. the man in the moon

2. Rahab hid the spies Joshua sent into Jericho and helped them escape. In return for her help, the spies promised Rahab that when Jericho fell down

    a. she and her family would be given riches

    b. she and her family would be left alive

    c. she would become queen of Israel

    d. she would star in movies

3. God promised Abraham that God would give him a son. How old was Abraham when his son Isaac was born?

    a. 20

    b. 30

    c. 50

    d. 100

4. God promised the people of Israel that a Messiah would come and deliver them from all their sins. That Messiah was

    a. John the Baptist

    b. Elijah

    c. Jesus

    d. Moses

5. When you make a promise to God, the Bible says you should fulfill it right away. Because God is not pleased with

    a. fools

    b. promise breakers

    c. daydreamers

    d. sinners

6. After Jesus rose from the dead and right before He ascended into heaven, "men dressed in white" promised His disciples that

    a. Jesus would rain down pennies from heaven

    b. they would speak before kings

    c. Jesus would come back the same way He left

    d. they would one day wear white

7. God promised Moses that on the night all the first-born of the Egyptians would die, the Israelites would be saved if they put blood on their doorposts. What was this event later called?

    a. Passover

    b. Pentecost

    c. Easter

    d. Epiphany

☆ ANSWERS ☆

1. a (Genesis 9:12–13)

2. b (Joshua 2:12–14)

3. d (Genesis 17:17)

4. c (Matthew 1:21)

5. a (Ecclesiastes 5:4–5)

6. c (Acts 1:11)

7. a (Exodus 12:12–13. Because God "passed over" the homes with the blood!)

⚡ QUIZ 25 ⚡

KINDNESS

(being good or nice to someone)

Joseph was part of the family God had promised to Abraham. The great grandson of Abraham, Joseph was also the favorite son of his father, Jacob. And Joseph liked being the favorite! Maybe it was when Jacob gave him a special, brightly colored coat that Joseph began to discover his older brothers didn't like him very much.

Being jealous causes people to make some very bad choices. And Joseph's brothers made some really bad choices. They sold their brother as a slave! Then they told their dad that Joseph had been killed by a wild animal. But God took the meanest trick Joseph's brothers ever played and turned it into a way to save many people from dying.

God made Joseph a ruler in his new land of Egypt. And Joseph made sure the Egyptians were ready for a time of famine, when no food would grow. People from other countries came to buy Egypt's food, and one day Joseph's brothers showed up. Instead of being angry, Joseph showed kindness and forgiveness to his brothers and praised God for making a plan that saved his family.

God wants you to be kind too. If you're not sure how to do that, maybe you'll get some ideas from the next quiz.

1. Years after Joseph's brothers sold him into slavery he showed kindness to them by
   a. giving them food
   b. giving them a meal at his house
   c. forgiving them for selling him into slavery
   d. all the above

2. When Paul and his companions were traveling around spreading the Good News about Jesus, Lydia heard them and became a believer. Then Lydia showed them kindness by
   a. washing their clothes
   b. inviting them to stay at her house
   c. giving them money
   d. serving them ice cream

3. After Jonathan died, his best friend David wanted to show kindness to Jonathan's family. David took Mephibosheth into his own family. Mephibosheth was Jonathan's
   a. father
   b. brother
   c. cousin
   d. son

4. Jesus once showed kindness to a widow who lived in a town called Nain. What did he do for her?
   a. find her a husband
   b. give her money
   c. raise her son from the dead
   d. buy her a puppy

5. In Jesus' story about being a good neighbor, the Good Samaritan showed kindness by

    a. taking care of the animals in his village

    b. helping a total stranger who had been beaten and robbed

    c. cleaning his neighbor's house

    d. washing his mayor's chariot

6. When the children of Israel wandered in the wilderness for 40 years, God showed them kindness by giving them *manna*. That name means

    a. what is it?

    b. God's gift

    c. white food

    d. is this rice?

7. When King Ahab's wicked wife, Jezebel, tried to kill all the prophets of God, Obadiah showed kindness to 100 of those prophets by

    a. giving them airline fare to fly home

    b. helping them find shields

    c. hiding them in caves and feeding them

    d. helping them secretly leave Israel

☆ ANSWERS ☆

1. d (Genesis 43:26–44:2; 45:4–8)

2. b (Acts 16:13–15)

3. d (2 Samuel 9:1–7)

4. c (Luke 7:11–15)

5. b (Luke 10:33–35)

6. a (Exodus 16:15)

7. c (1 Kings 18:13)

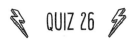

QUIZ 26

LEADERSHIP

(being in charge; showing by example how to do good things)

Joshua learned how to lead from Moses. When Moses could no longer lead the people to the land God promised to give them, Joshua took over. He was a good example to God's people.

God said He had a special way for Joshua to win a battle against a town called Jericho. God wanted the people to walk around the town walls. When the time was right, they would blow trumpets. You might not think something like that would work, but when the people obeyed, the walls of Jericho came down. God's plans always work.

Sometimes the people forgot it was God who helped them. Some decided to stop following God. Joshua told them, "Choose today whom you will serve. . . . As for me and my family, we will serve the Lord" (Joshua 24:15).

The best thing Moses taught Joshua was that the best leaders follow God. The best thing Joshua did was agree with Moses. With God's help and Joshua's leadership, God's people finally came home.

Joshua led by example because he learned by example. God is pleased when we're brave enough to show others what it looks like to follow Him.

Want to be a good leader? See what you can learn about leadership from the people in the quiz that follows.

1. Moses sent 12 spies into Canaan to see if the Israelites could successfully take over their Promised Land. The two spies who said, "Yes, we can," were named
   a. Bert and Ernie
   b. Jonathan and David
   c. Abraham and Isaac
   d. Joshua and Caleb

2. After Saul became a follower of Christ, the other disciples were still afraid of him. Who showed leadership by welcoming the man who once tried to hurt the church?
   a. Barnabas
   b. Tertius
   c. Onesimus
   d. Agabus

3. When God told Solomon to ask for anything he wanted, Solomon asked for _____ so he could be a good king and leader of his people.
   a. a queen
   b. a throne
   c. a palace
   d. understanding

4. Nicodemus, who came to see Jesus secretly at night, was a member of the Jewish ruling council called the Sanhedrin. Nicodemus was also
   a. a leper
   b. blind
   c. a Pharisee
   d. a spy

5. When John was in exile on the Island of Patmos, he saw visions of things to come. One of those visions was about the armies of heaven. And the leader of those armies was
   a. John himself
   b. Jesus the King of kings
   c. Michael the archangel
   d. the apostle Peter

6. When Paul encouraged Timothy as a church leader, what did the apostle say people should not disrespect about Timothy?
   a. that he was short
   b. that he was poor
   c. that he was sickly
   d. that he was young

7. The only woman who was a judge (or leader) of Israel was
   a. Mary
   b. Deborah
   c. Eve
   d. Martha

☆ ANSWERS ☆

1. d (Numbers 13:16, 30)

2. a (Acts 9:26–30)

3. d (1 Kings 3:7–9)

4. c (John 3:1–2)

5. b (Revelation 19:11–16)

6. d (1 Timothy 4:12)

7. b (Judges 4:4)

QUIZ 27

LEARNING

(getting to know someone or something)

Kaboo was a Liberian prince. He was a prisoner of a nearby tribe. He was kidnapped and beaten nearly every day.

His family tried but couldn't free him. One day Kaboo saw a bright light and heard a voice telling him to run. The ropes holding his arms together fell off. Although Kaboo was sick, he was free.

Kaboo was fourteen when he escaped. He found work at a coffee plantation. There he learned about Jesus. He was certain Jesus freed him. People needed to know Jesus.

This young man became known as Samuel Morris. He worked on a ship to come to America. The very first night in America, Samuel shared what he knew about Jesus, and twenty people became Christians.

God was able to use Samuel to share His love. Samuel wanted to learn everything he could about Jesus so he could return to Liberia and share God's Good News.

Samuel went to college, learned about Jesus, and led people to Jesus. When he was twenty, Samuel became sick. He didn't make it home to Liberia. He said, "I have finished my job. [God] will send others better than I to do the work in Africa." And God did.

Learning is good—and fun! Let's see what you learn from this quiz.

1. Which of the following is *not* a time Moses told the Israelites to teach God's Word to their kids?
   a. when you sit
   b. when you go swimming
   c. when you lie down
   d. when you walk on the road

2. Priscilla and her husband Aquila taught this person more things about God:
   a. Amos
   b. Adam
   c. Apollos
   d. Absalom

3. According to the book of Proverbs, what kind of person grows in learning?
   a. wise
   b. wealthy
   c. winsome
   d. wonderful

4. What powerful country sent the young Jewish men Daniel, Shadrach, Meshach, and Abednego to school in order to serve its king?
   a. Assyria
   b. Greece
   c. Babylon
   d. Russia

5. Samuel's mother dedicated Samuel to the Lord. Then she brought Samuel to the Temple so he could learn
   a. to serve and worship the Lord
   b. to be the next king
   c. to tend the priests' sheep
   d. to play the harp

6. When Jesus was 12, Mary and Joseph found Him in the temple sitting among the teachers listening to them and asking them questions. The Bible says that Jesus grew
   a. in mind
   b. in body
   c. in favor with God and men
   d. all the above

7. Martha's sister Mary learned from Jesus because she sat at His feet and
   a. listened to Him speak
   b. read her Bible
   c. asked Him questions
   d. tuned in a podcast

☆ ANSWERS ☆

1. b (Deuteronomy 6:7. But you could learn God's Word even then!)

2. c (Acts 18:24–26)

3. a (Proverbs 1:5)

4. c (Daniel 1:3–7)

5. a (1 Samuel 1:28)

6. d (Luke 2:52)

7. a (Luke 10:39)

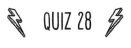

QUIZ 28

Love

(selfless concern for others)

Ben Carson was angry. His father left his family when he was young. He didn't think that was fair. His mother was sent to the hospital because she was so sad. That wasn't what Ben had planned or wanted. He attended many different schools. Sometimes people were unkind.

It was only when Ben let God help that he began to change for the better. He learned about love, forgiveness, and compassion.

God replaced Ben's angry heart with one that could show love. Ben discovered he wanted to help others instead of hurting them. When he grew up, he believed the best way he could help was to become a doctor. And he was a good one. People noticed him.

Ben began to write books. He was asked to speak to large groups of people. When he retired as a doctor, the president of the United States gave him a job. Ben Carson learned how to give a soft answer in a sharp-word world.

You can show your love for God by serving Him. And you can show your love for others by helping them. Let's find out what you know about love from this next quiz.

1. According to the book of Romans, how did God prove His love for the world?
   a. by creating the sunshine
   b. by providing the Bible
   c. by putting a rainbow in the sky
   d. by sending Jesus to die for sinners

2. God the Father's love is so great through Jesus that we should be called
   a. God's children
   b. Christians
   c. churchgoers
   d. God's creation

3. Jacob loved and wanted to marry Rachel. But Rachel's father, Laban, tricked Jacob into marrying her sister
   a. Ruth
   b. Mary
   c. Leah
   d. Esther

4. Jesus said that the first and greatest instruction in the law was
   a. love the Lord your God with all your heart, soul and mind
   b. be kind and loving to strangers who may be angels
   c. love and obey your parents and things will go well
   d. eat your brussels sprouts

5. The book of Proverbs says that hate starts fights, but that love covers all
   a. people
   b. sins
   c. enemies
   d. friends

6. According to Jesus, what would Christians' love for each other prove to everyone else?
   a. that they are His followers
   b. that they should be respected
   c. that they know what is right
   d. that they will change the world

7. According to the book of 1 John, what is something that Christians are *not* supposed to love?
   a. scary movies
   b. bad language
   c. expensive clothing
   d. the world or anything in it

☆ ANSWERS ☆

1. d (Romans 5:8)

2. a (1 John 3:1)

3. c (Genesis 29:16–25. That's not a good situation.)

4. a (Matthew 22:37–38)

5. b (Proverbs 10:12)

6. a (John 13:34–35)

7. d (1 John 2:15)

QUIZ 29

MEEKNESS

(being quiet and self-controlled)

Tim Tebow was a fantastic football player in high school. He was an amazing football player in college. He proved he could play football in the National Football League. But he was let go from one team and then another. Pretty soon no team wanted to hire him.

Baseball was also one of Tim's favorite sports, so he tried that. He hasn't made the major leagues, but he has played on some lower level professional teams. His first at bat was a home run, but he doesn't hit home runs every time.

It's rare to see Tim upset. He continues to work hard because he wants to please his Boss—God. Tim's meekness has been an inspiration to others who also want to do God's will. When Tim's not on the field, he might be serving God in other ways. He has given and helped raise money for an orphanage, a hospital, disadvantaged kids, and kids with cancer.

When you work for God, *He* gets to choose what you do. And you'll enjoy it a lot more if you do it with the right attitude. Let's look at some people whose meekness helped them find their way to doing what God wanted them to do.

1. Meekness means serving others with loving patience and self-control. Ruth showed her meekness in her attitude toward her mother-in-law
   a. Eve
   b. Esther
   c. Naomi
   d. Rachel

2. Job showed meekness through all his sufferings by saying he would trust God even if God _____ him.
   a. forgot
   b. killed
   c crushed
   d. fought

3. Moses is an excellent example of meekness because of the way he dealt with the grumbling of the children of Israel as they wandered in the wilderness for _____ years.
   a. 10
   b. 20
   c. 30
   d. 40

4. Jesus is the greatest example of meekness. Even though the soldiers nailed Him to the cross, Jesus said, "Father, forgive them for they. . .
   a. do not know what they are doing"
   b. don't really mean to kill Me"
   c. have no idea who I am"
   d. are ignorant Romans"

5. In the Sermon on the Mount, Jesus said people who are meek or have no pride are
   a. hopeful
   b. happy
   c. human
   d. hearty

6. In the book of Galatians (KJV), the apostle Paul says that meekness is a
   a. good thing
   b. bad thing
   c. fruit of the Spirit
   d. a lesson to be learned

7. Jesus says you should follow His teachings and learn from Him. Because He is meek, what will you find with Him?
   a. joy in your home
   b. hope for your future
   c. wisdom for your exams
   d. rest for your soul

☆ ANSWERS ☆

1. c (Ruth 1:14-15)

2. b (Job 13:15)

3. d (Numbers 32:13)

4. a (Luke 23:34)

5. b (Matthew 5:5. Some Bible translations say "blessed.")

6. c (Galatians 5:22-23)

7. d (Matthew 11:29)

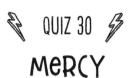

QUIZ 30

MERCY

(kindness by one who has power over another)

Samson was the world's strongest man. He could lift, carry, and pull more than anyone. But Samson didn't work out in a gym. He didn't always eat the right food. He wasn't a superhero. Samson was strong because God made him strong. God also made him brave.

Samson fought those who fought his family. As a judge, he made decisions for the people. But in his own life, Samson often made very bad choices.

One day a pretty girl named Delilah was hired by Samson's enemies to learn how to make Samson weak. She tricked Samson into telling her his secret. God had told him that he should never cut his hair. Some might think Samson was strong because he had long hair. But the truth is Samson was strong because he obeyed God.

When Samson fell asleep, Delilah shaved off his hair. And when Samson woke up, his strength was gone. His enemies took him away and made him a slave. Because his strength was gone, he couldn't escape, fight, or run.

As the days passed, Samson's hair grew back. God was making him strong again. Samson remembered why he needed to obey. He prayed to God to give him back his strength and God showed mercy to him.

Now let's see what *you* know about God's mercy—and showing mercy to others.

1. While Samson was a slave in prison, God showed mercy to him by letting his hair grow back and giving Samson back
    a. his dignity
    b. his strength
    c. his sight
    d. his pride

2. In the parable of the Pharisee and the tax collector, the Pharisee bragged about himself but the tax collector asked God to have pity or mercy on him because he was
    a. a sinner
    b. a good man
    c. a father of ten
    d. a friend of Jesus

3. God said He would show mercy to how many generations of the people that love Him and keep His commandments?
    a. 13
    b. 52
    c. hundreds
    d. thousands

4. In the Sermon on the Mount, Jesus said, "Blessed are the merciful (KJV)" because they will be shown
    a. love
    b. peace
    c. mercy
    d. off

5. Jesus showed mercy to a man that was possessed by many evil spirits. Jesus made the evil spirits leave the man and go into a nearby
    a. flock of doves
    b. flock of sheep
    c. herd of pigs
    d. herd of cows

6. As Jesus and His disciples were leaving Jericho one day, two blind beggars begged Jesus to have mercy on them. Jesus stopped and
    a. gave them money
    b. gave them new clothes
    c. gave them their sight
    d. all the above

7. God says He will have mercy on whom?
    a. anyone He wants to
    b. those who really need it
    c. anyone who gives money to church
    d. those who get to Him first

☆ ANSWERS ☆

1. b (Judges 16:21–30)

2. a (Luke 18:13)

3. d (Exodus 20:6)

4. c (Matthew 5:7)

5. c (Mark 5:1–13)

6. c (Matthew 20:29–34)

7. a (Romans 9:15–16)

QUIZ 31

NEARNESS TO GOD

(really knowing God personally)

George Müller ran several orphanages in London. Children who stayed with George always had meals, a place to stay, and a godly example. Yet when he was growing up, George had stolen money from his dad, cheated, lied, and gambled.

God changed George. The closer he got to God, the less interested he was in asking help from anyone else. He said about God, "If you walk with Him and look to Him, and expect help from Him, He will never fail you."

Through others, God brought George food, milk, and money for his orphanages when it was needed most. Once when he was traveling across the ocean to go to an important meeting, fog rolled in and the captain of the ship told him he wouldn't make it to the meeting. George prayed with the captain. When the captain looked again, the fog was gone!

George lived every day knowing God would take care of getting done what needed to be done.

Some think the best way to do things is to work as hard as they can and then ask for God's help when it gets too hard. God wants to be given the chance to help in every situation, from beginning to end. He always handles things better than we can.

Let's see what help God can give you in solving this quiz!

1. Hagar ran away when Sarah was being mean to her. When Hagar was all alone in the wilderness, the Lord came to her and blessed her. Hagar called the Lord "the God who. . ."

    a. sees
    b. remembers
    c. surrounds
    d. loves

2. God gave Jacob a dream of a ladder that reached from earth to heaven. On the ladder, going up and down, were

    a. sheep
    b. people
    c. angels
    d. firefighters

3. When God told Abraham He was going to destroy Sodom and Gomorrah, Abraham felt close enough to God to ask Him to spare the city if God could find at least _____ righteous people there.

    a. 1,000
    b. 300
    c. 64
    d. 10

4. Enoch is an Old Testament character who was so close to God that he

    a. was taken straight to heaven
    b. wrote the book of Judges
    c. turned water into wine
    d. parted the Jordan River

5. When Jesus appeared in His glory to John on the Island of Patmos, John immediately fell down at Jesus' feet as if he were

   a. overjoyed
   b. dead
   c. struck blind
   d. fainting

6. When Jesus appeared to Mary Magdalene after His resurrection, she didn't recognize Him at first. She thought He was

   a. an angel
   b. the undertaker
   c. the gardener
   d. a tourist

7. Anna was so close to God that she knew Jesus, the Messiah, would come in her lifetime. To be sure she didn't miss seeing Him, Anna spent every day fasting and praying

   a. at home
   b. at the city gate
   c. in the temple
   d. at Mary and Martha's house

☆ ANSWERS ☆

1. a (Genesis 16:13)

2. c (Genesis 28:12)

3. d (Genesis 18:32) (The cities were
   destroyed and the only people who
   escaped were Lot, his wife, and his
   two daughters.)

4. a (Genesis 5:24)

5. b (Revelation 1:17)

6. c (John 20:15)

7. c (Luke 2:36–38)

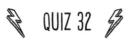

QUIZ 32

OBEDIENCE

(doing as you're told)

The Bible tells of three young men—Shadrach, Meshach, and Abednego—who followed God. They had been born in Israel, but were captured and taken to Babylon.

The people of Babylon didn't follow God. One time, their king, Nebuchadnezzar, had a large idol made. He said people had to bow down to it whenever the musicians started playing. When the music stopped, everyone could go back to what they were doing. If they didn't bow, it was game over for them.

Shadrach, Meshach, and Abednego wouldn't bow to the king's idol. Thinking they may have misunderstood his law, the king gave them a second chance, but the three men still refused. That made the king mad. He made his large furnace seven times hotter than usual, and his soldiers threw the three men inside. But they didn't die or burn, because God saved them.

Finally, King Nebuchadnezzar did the right thing. He praised God and told the three to come out of the flames. They may have worked for a king, but they served God.

Like Shadrach, Meshach, and Abednego, you too serve the true God. Let's see how much you know about obedience—and disobedience—as you try the quiz that follows.

1. Peter and the other apostles told the members of the Sanhedrin, "We must obey God instead of. . ."
   a. you
   b. men
   c. Satan
   d. idols

2. What did Jesus say was true when we obey His teaching?
   a. we are His followers for sure
   b. we love Him
   c. we live in His love
   d. all the above

3. The book of Hebrews says even Jesus learned to obey by what?
   a. His mother's teaching
   b. time spent in the temple
   c. suffering
   d. reading good books

4. The apostle Paul said he worked hard to make his _____ obey him.
   a. dog
   b. church
   c. fellow missionaries
   d. body

5. What were the disciples surprised to see obeying Jesus?

a. animals and birds
b. wind and waves
c. sun and moon
d. clouds and lightning

6. Who did Esther obey when he told her she needed to talk to the king and save her people?

a. Bigthan
b. Hathach
c. Mordecai
d. the angel Gabriel

7. Samuel told King Saul, "To obey is better than _____"

a. love
b. wisdom
c. riches
d. sacrifice

☆ ANSWERS ☆

1. b (Acts 5:29)

2. d (John 8:31; John 14:21; John 15:10)

3. c (Hebrews 5:8)

4. d (1 Corinthians 9:27)

5. b (Matthew 8:27)

6. c (Esther 4:13–14)

7. d (1 Samuel 15:22 KJV)

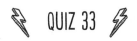

QUIZ 33

PEACEMAKING

(keeping others calm and quiet)

William Wilberforce grew up in a family that loved Jesus. William learned about Jesus but never really followed Him as a child. He was confused about the things he was told, and he liked making bad choices.

As a young man, William got involved in British politics. He soon discovered he needed to know Jesus. That's when he began his lifelong journey.

Many members of Parliament (a part of the British government) thought being a Christian made a person unfit for politics. They made fun of William and wanted him to leave. But he didn't. He actually relied on his new love for Jesus to help him stand up for truth, the poor, and freeing slaves.

William helped stop the slave trade in England. It didn't happen overnight. Many years would pass before William saw real change.

William wanted to follow God's Word. He once said, "What a difference it would be if our system of morality were based on the Bible." He knew the only way to help make peace on this earth was to worship God and do His will.

Maybe you will have the chance to be a peacemaker. Let's find out what the Bible says about it.

1. In the Sermon on the Mount, Jesus said peacemakers are blessed and will be called
  a. a blessing
  b. happy
  c. children of God
  d. awesome

2. Abraham and his nephew, Lot, both had so many flocks and herds that their herdsmen fought each other trying to get the best land for their master's animals. To make peace, Abraham and Lot
  a. moved away from each other
  b. sold their animals
  c. hired new herdsmen
  d. offered their animals to God

3. The book of Romans says that you should live in peace with everyone. . .
  a. whenever they're nice to you
  b. as much as you can
  c. to earn your way to heaven
  d. even if they're real jerks

4. To keep David from killing her foolish husband, Nabal's wife, Abigail, made peace by
  a. telling David to blame her instead
  b. bringing David and his men food and drink
  c. asking David to forgive her
  d. all the above

5. The book of James says that God's wisdom from _____ is first pure, then gives peace.
a. Moses
b. Paul
c. the temple
d. heaven

6. What does the Bible's longest chapter—Psalm 119—say gives great peace?
a. ten hours of sleep a night
b. loving God's law
c. serving as a foreign missionary
d. playing hymns on a harp

7. How does the book of Philippians describe God's peace?
a. "as high as the heavens"
b. "stronger than a lion"
c. "greater than the human mind can understand"
d. all the above

☆ ANSWERS ☆

1. b (Matthew 5:9)

2. a (Genesis 13:9)

3. b (Romans 12:18. By the way, answer C is *totally* wrong—nobody can earn their way to heaven. That's why we need Jesus!)

4. d (1 Samuel 25:18–28)

5. d (James 3:17)

6. b (Psalm 119:165)

7. c (Philippians 4:7)

QUIZ 34

PRAYER

(asking God to use His power)

Do you pray to God? Do you ever wonder if He's listening or if you're even saying the words right? Everybody feels that way sometimes.

Hezekiah was a king in Judah. If anyone had a reason to wonder if he were praying the right way, it was Hezekiah.

He opened the temple, and the priests spoke only about the true God. The people were invited to follow God again.

Hezekiah was still learning about God when enemy soldiers came and said they were taking over. This is when Hezekiah learned more about prayer. He read what God said in His Word. He wanted to speak to God about what his nation was going through. He prayed, asking God to save the people in his kingdom.

There was no reason anyone should have expected the people of Judah to stay safe from their enemy, but God answered Hezekiah's prayer by protecting the people.

Praying to God is something you can do. It's something you *should* do.

Here are some things about prayer and examples of how other people pray.

1. When the Assyrian army surrounded Jerusalem, King Hezekiah and the prophet Isaiah prayed that God would deliver them. That night God answered their prayer by

    a. blinding the Assyrian soldiers

    b. sending His angel to kill 185,000 Assyrian soldiers

    c. causing the earth to open up and swallow the army

    d. making killer bees chase the Assyrians away

2. What did the Jews under Queen Esther add to their prayers for her safety?

    a. skipping meals for three days and nights

    b. singing psalms

    c. giving a special offering

    d. dancing a waltz

3. When Jesus was in the Garden of Gethsemane right before He was arrested, He prayed so hard that

    a. He got a headache

    b. God took Him up to heaven

    c. an army of angels landed in the garden

    d. He sweat drops like blood

4. On Mount Carmel, Elijah showed the prophets of Baal that God is the only God. Elijah prayed and

    a. God sent fire from heaven

    b. the skin of the prophets turned purple

    c. the prophets of Baal dropped dead

    d. worms ate King Ahab

5. The prophet Elijah once prayed for rain. How many times did he send his servant to look toward the sea and see if the rain was starting to fall?

    a. 2

    b. 4

    c. 6

    d. 7

6. In the Sermon on the Mount, how did Jesus describe prayer?

    a. "ask and it will be given to you"

    b. "seek and you will find"

    c. "knock and the door will be opened to you"

    d. all the above

7. The book of 1 Thessalonians says you are to pray

    a. every night before bed

    b. only on Sundays

    c. without stopping

    d. only in church

☆ ANSWERS ☆

1. b (2 Kings 19:35)

2. a (Esther 4:15–16)

3. d (Luke 22:44)

4. a (1 Kings 18:38)

5. d (1 Kings 18:41–44)

6. d (Matthew 7:7 KJV)

7. c (1 Thessalonians 5:17)

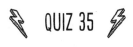

QUIETNESS

(being calm and at peace)

Samuel was an answer to prayer. His mom, Hannah, had prayed for a son, promising God to give the boy back to Him. So God gave her Samuel. The young boy grew close to his mom, but one day she took Samuel to the temple to give her son back to God. She wanted this gift of a child to be used by God. And God did use Samuel. "The boy served the Lord with Eli the religious leader" (1 Samuel 2:11).

God spoke to young Samuel one night when he was lying quietly in bed. (You have to be quiet to hear the voice of God.) Samuel didn't recognize God's voice at first, but Eli realized God was calling him. Eli told Samuel to lie down and see if God called again. When God did, Samuel said, "Speak, for Your servant is listening" (1 Samuel 3:10).

God kept talking to Samuel. Samuel listened and told others what God had said. Samuel had to speak with courage because people did not always want to hear what God had to say.

Let's see what else you can learn about being quiet and listening to God.

1. What did the apostle Peter say a quiet spirit does for a woman?
   a. it makes her strong
   b. it makes her rich
   c. it makes her happy
   d. it makes her beautiful

2. The Proverbs say a piece of dry bread with quietness is better than a great feast with
   a. fighting
   b. loud music
   c. too much talk
   d. police sirens

3. In the book of Psalms, God tells us to be still and quiet and know
   a. He is strong
   b. He is God
   c. He is good
   d. He is mighty

4. God told the people of Israel, "Your strength will come by being quiet and. . ."
   a. trusting God
   b. singing in the choir
   c. imitating Moses
   d. lifting weights

5. Who did God speak to in a "still small voice"?

    a. Paul

    b. Moses

    c. David

    d. Elijah

6. Paul told the people in Thessalonica to learn how to be quiet, to mind their own business, and to work with. . .

    a. mom and dad

    b. their classmates

    c. their own hands

    d. people they like

7. The Shepherd in Psalm 23 leads His sheep (who are a symbol of His followers) beside "quiet waters" to

    a. keep them safe from wolves

    b. restore their strength

    c. keep them from falling off a cliff

    d. feed them

☆ ANSWERS ☆

1. d (1 Peter 3:4)

2. a (Proverbs 17:1)

3. b (Psalm 46:10 KJV)

4. a (Isaiah 30:15)

5. d (1 Kings 19:9-13 KJV)

6. c (1 Thessalonians 4:11 KJV)

7. b (Psalm 23:3)

RESISTING TEMPTATION

**(choosing what God wants you to
do over what you want to do)**

Eric Liddell was a very good runner. He was known as the fastest runner in his home country of Scotland.

The leader of his school said that Eric never seemed proud or demanding. He demonstrated what it looked like to follow James 4:10: "Let yourself be brought low before the Lord. Then He will lift you up and help you."

In 1924, Eric went to the Olympics in Paris. One of the events was happening on Sunday—and it was his best event. Would he run? Eric believed God meant what He said in Deuteronomy 5:12: "Remember the Day of Rest, to keep it holy, as the Lord your God told you." Eric believed Sunday was this day. So he did *not* run.

Instead, Eric ran another race on another day and won. God was honored. A year later, Eric became a missionary in China. This was another way to honor God.

Eric knew what was most important. He said, "Each one of us is in a greater race than any I have run in Paris, and this race ends when God gives out the medals." That is the race of a lifetime.

Let's see what more you can learn that will help you to run from temptation.

1. When Potiphar's wife tried to tempt Joseph, he
   a. kindly said no
   b. ran away
   c. screamed
   d. called the police

2. When Satan tempted Jesus, He resisted the devil by doing what?
   a. singing hymns
   b. quoting scripture
   c. performing miracles
   d. sticking His fingers in His ears

3. The Bible says all people are tempted by the same types of things, but you can resist any temptation because God
   a. will forgive you
   b. will bless you
   c. will ignore it
   d. will show you a way to escape it

4. What did the serpent tell Eve she would get by disobeying God in the Garden of Eden?
   a. she would live forever
   b. she would be like God, knowing good and evil
   c. she would be beautiful and rich
   d. she would be the boss over Adam

5. Jesus told His disciples they could resist temptation by watching and
   a. waiting
   b. hoping
   c. learning
   d. praying

6. The Bible says money leads many people into temptation. What exactly is the problem with money?
   a. having too much
   b. having too little
   c. loving it
   d. burning it

7. When Paul and Silas were beaten and thrown into prison, they fought the temptation to moan and complain. Instead they
   a. sang
   b. prayed
   c. cried
   d. a and b

☆ ANSWERS ☆

1. b (Genesis 39:7–12)

2. c (Matthew 4:7)

3. d (1 Corinthians 10:13)

4. b (Genesis 3:1-6)

5. d (Matthew 26:41)

6. c (1 Timothy 6:9–10)

7. d (Acts 16:25)

QUIZ 37

Respect

(to show honor)

Jesus died on a cross in the afternoon. The sky was dark, and the hill where Jesus was crucified was silent. It was a strange and sad ending to His life. He healed and helped, fixed and forgave, taught and trained. *Now?* He was dead.

Joseph was a rich man from the city of Arimathea. He was a religious leader who noticed Jesus still hanging on the cross. So Joseph went to see the governor, Pilate. Joseph asked for Jesus' body so he could give Him a proper burial. Pilate agreed.

Joseph took the body down from the cross and placed it in his own new tomb. It seemed the right thing to do. But Jesus didn't stay in the grave very long. He died on Friday, but by Sunday He'd risen from the dead!

Joseph was called "good and just." He'd quietly followed Jesus, but when no one came to show respect to Jesus after He died, Joseph did what needed to be done.

There would be no applause or thanks from the people who watched Jesus die. But Joseph's kindness must have meant something special to God, because Joseph's generous gift is mentioned in the books of Matthew, Mark, Luke, and John.

Now, let's see what you know about showing or getting respect.

1. Who helped Joseph of Arimathea take Jesus' body from the cross and move it to the tomb?

a. Peter
b. James and John
c. Nicodemus
d. Zaccheus

2. A Shunammite woman showed respect and hospitality to Elisha by adding a room onto her house just for him. In return for her kindness, God granted the woman's deepest desire, which was

a. to have more money
b. to live to be 100
c. to have a child
d. to buy more clothes

3. In the book of Ephesians, the apostle Paul says that you are to obey and respect

a. your mom and dad
b. your Sunday school teachers
c. your sports coaches
d. your president and congress

4. The book of Acts says that God is "no respecter of persons" (KJV). In this case, this means that God

a. is so much greater, He doesn't need to respect anyone else
b. offers salvation to every person, no matter their background
c. tells people to respect themselves
d. is a respecter of animals only

5. Some youths showed disrespect to the prophet Elisha by mocking him and calling him
a. a baby
b. a yellow belly
c. a worm
d. bald head

6. According to the book of Leviticus, how should younger people show respect to the elderly?
a. by buying them groceries
b. by standing in their presence
c. by kissing their cheeks
d. by giving them a salute

7. What does the apostle Paul say good church leaders are worthy of?
a. twice as much pay
b. smiles and hugs
c. kind words and compliments
d. three weeks of vacation

☆ ANSWERS ☆

1. c (John 19:38–40)

2. c (2 Kings 4:15–16)

3. a (Ephesians 6:1–2)

4. b (Acts 10:34)

5. d (2 Kings 2:23 KJV. The kids got mauled by bears for their disrespect!)

6. b (Leviticus 19:32 KJV)

7. a (1 Timothy 5:17)

⚡ QUIZ 38 ⚡

RESPONSIBILITY

(your duties)

God has something big in mind that only you can do. But before you do that big thing, God may want to see if you will do *small* things well. That might mean making sure you obey when a parent tells you to keep your room clean or take out the garbage. That's called being responsible.

Nehemiah's job was making sure that what the king drank wasn't poisoned. That was an important job, but Nehemiah learned of a bigger one: he heard the walls of Jerusalem had been torn down. The people living in the city weren't protected. No one was trying to rebuild. No one had enough money to do this big job.

Nehemiah prayed, asking that the king might help rebuild the walls. When Nehemiah asked the king, he said he would help. He even paid for it! When Nehemiah got to Jerusalem, the people living there helped—even when mean bullies made fun of them. In a very short time, the city walls were rebuilt, God was honored, and those men who had made fun of Nehemiah couldn't believe their eyes.

When God needs something done, He will get it done. He will use people who did a good job doing small things first. That way the big things won't seem so hard.

What can you learn about responsibility from the examples that follow?

1. How long did it take, under Nehemiah's responsible leadership, for the walls of Jerusalem to be rebuilt?
    a. a week
    b. 52 days
    c. 3 years
    d. a decade

2. Why did Abigail have to take responsibility for her foolish husband's actions?
    a. he had let his roof collapse
    b. he had gambled away his money
    c. he had insulted David and his soldiers
    d. he had let his cows escape their pasture

3. What did Mordecai tell Esther to encourage her to risk herself to save the Jews?
    a. "The Lord your God will fight for you"
    b. "Be strong and have much strength of heart"
    c. "You must not worship any other god"
    d. "Who knows if you have not become queen for such a time as this?"

4. In Jesus' "parable of the talents" (or "story of the three servants and the money"), why was the third servant punished?
    a. he stole some of the money he'd been given
    b. he didn't earn as much money as the other two servants
    c. he didn't even try to earn more money with what he'd been given
    d. a and c

5. When Naomi urged her widowed daughters-in-law, Orpah and Ruth, to return to their own people, Ruth felt it was her responsibility to

    a. leave Naomi as she'd said
    b. go live with Orpah
    c. find herself a husband
    d. stay with Naomi and help her

6. When Jesus forgave Peter for saying he didn't even know Him, what did Jesus tell Peter his responsibility would be?

    a. "Take care of My sheep"
    b. "Set up the worship tent"
    c. "Sing with joy to the Lord"
    d. "Build an ark"

7. As He hung on the cross, who did Jesus select for the responsibility of taking care of His mother, Mary?

    a. Nicodemus
    b. Mary Magdalene
    c. Peter and Andrew
    d. John

☆ ANSWERS ☆

1. b (Nehemiah 6:15)

2. c (1 Samuel 25:23–31)

3. d (Esther 4:14)

4. c (Matthew 25:14–30)

5. d (Ruth 1:16–18)

6. a (John 21:16–17)

7. d (John 19:26–27. When he wrote, John called himself, "the follower whom [Jesus] loved.")

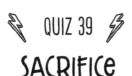

QUIZ 39

SACRIFICE

(the giving up of something)

Not every story seems happy. Bad things happen to people every day. Understanding why can be hard.

John Stam followed Jesus—all the way to China as a missionary. His wife, Betty, lived in China. She was the daughter of missionaries. Together they started their ministry. Together they shared God's Good News. Together they had a daughter named Helen.

Early in December 1934, John and Betty looked forward to Helen's first Christmas. That's when the young family was surprised. Members of the Chinese Red Army came into their home, demanded their money, and kidnapped them.

They were taken to the city jail. A note was discovered—it included a verse that showed that John was ready to live or die. The note never made it out of China. John and Betty never returned home. Two days later, the soldiers killed the missionary couple. Betty had hidden their daughter, Helen. She was later rescued.

A story like the Stams' is sad, but it has helped many people over many years become missionaries and serve God. God always gets the last word. He blesses sacrifices made on His behalf. And God stands with those who hurt—Psalm 34:18 says that God "is near to those who have a broken heart. And He saves those who are broken in spirit."

Here's a quiz to help you learn more about what sacrifice means.

1. What did Moses give up to become the leader of God's people, the Israelites?
   a. being known as Pharaoh's grandson
   b. the riches of Egypt
   c. the pleasures of sin
   d. all the above

2. When God told Abraham to sacrifice his son, Isaac, Abraham showed faith by preparing to do it. But God stopped Abraham from killing Isaac and provided a _____ to be sacrificed instead.
   a. donkey
   b. goat
   c. ram
   d. bull

3. Who was the first of the twelve disciples to sacrifice his life (or become a "martyr") for Jesus?
   a. Matthew
   b. Bartholomew
   c. James
   d. Andrew

4. When God accepted Abel's animal sacrifice but rejected Cain's sacrifice of fruits and vegetables, how did Cain respond?
   a. he started raising sheep
   b. he stopped making sacrifices at all
   c. he killed Abel
   d. he argued with God for hours

5. How did Jesus describe the everyday sacrifices we must make to follow Him?
- a. "take up your cross"
- b. "lay down your dreams"
- c. "put off every weight"
- d. "just say no"

6. According to the apostle Paul, why did Jesus—who was rich in heaven—become poor here on earth?
- a. to set a good example
- b. because earth money is dirty
- c. so we could become rich
- d. to make the poor feel better about themselves

7. According to Jesus, what is the greatest example of love for others?
- a. to give all your money
- b. to lay down your life
- c. to spend all your time
- d. to hand over your food

☆ ANSWERS ☆

1. d (Hebrews 11:24–26)

2. c (Genesis 22:13)

3. c (Acts 12:1–2)

4. c (Genesis 4:3–8)

5. a (Matthew 16:24)

6. c (2 Corinthians 8:9)

7. b (John 15:13)

⚡ QUIZ 40 ⚡

SELF-DENIAL

(giving up your own interests and needs)

Dietrich Bonhoeffer was a pastor in Germany during World War II. He believed what he read in Galatians 3:28: "God does not see you as a Jew or as a Greek. . . . He does not see you as a man or as a woman. You are all one in Christ."

Dietrich heard German leaders saying mean things about Jewish people and stirring up hatred against them. As a Christian, Dietrich knew that God loved the Jews—in fact, Jesus was Jewish! So he spoke out, for the Jews and against the German government treating them badly.

It was a brave thing to do because the German leaders arrested and killed Dietrich Bonhoeffer. He denied himself to obey what God told him to do.

It may be hard to deny yourself and do what's right. But if that's what God asks you to do, that is what you must do. And you can be sure God will be with you.

Let's see what more we can find out about the Bible's teachings on self-denial.

1. When Jesus said, "If anyone wants to be My follower, he must give up himself and his own desires," how did He finish the statement?
    a. "he must put a lot of money in the offering plate"
    b. "he must take up his cross and follow Me"
    c. "he must pray for the strength to continue"
    d. "he must smile even when they feel like frowning"

2. What did Peter, James, and John give up to become disciples or "followers" of Jesus?
    a. a house and garage
    b. two fishing boats
    c. three bags of money
    d. everything they had

3. Jesus said, "If any man comes to Me and does not have much more love for Me than for his father and mother. . .brothers and sisters, and even his own life, he cannot be _____."
    a. My friend
    b. My son
    c. My follower
    d. My helper

4. What could Queen Esther have lost by asking King Xerxes to save her people, the Jews?
    a. her crown
    b. her reputation
    c. her life
    d. her best friend

5. What did Jesus say you should do to your hand or foot if it "causes you to stumble"—meaning, if you want to do something wrong with it?

    a. tie it down
    b. cut it off
    c. tell it to stop
    d. tattoo it

6. How did a widow in a town called Zarephath deny herself to help the prophet Elijah?

    a. she gave him the last of her food
    b. she gave him the last of her money
    c. she gave him her horse and wagon
    d. she gave him her only child

7. What does the Bible say we should "walk by" to keep from doing the things our body wants us to do?

    a. the Spirit
    b. the Ten Commandments
    c. the Psalms
    d. the Cross

☆ ANSWERS ☆

1. b (Mark 8:34)

2. d (Luke 5:11)

3. c (Luke 14:26)

4. c (Esther 4:10–11)

5. b (Matthew 18:8. Jesus probably didn't
   mean you should *really* cut off your
   hand or foot—but He wanted people to
   know how important it is to say no
   to sin!)

6. a (1 Kings 17:7–16)

7. a (Galatians 5:16 KJV)

service

(the act of helping someone)

Moses was adopted as the grandson of Pharaoh. The plan was for Moses to live in the palace for the rest of his life. This was not God's plan.

When Moses was forty, he killed a man who was hurting a fellow Hebrew. Then Moses ran away. For forty years, he lived in the wilderness caring for sheep. He was married there. His sons were born there. He enjoyed the quiet. But that would end, for God had a plan.

One day God asked Moses to leave the sheep behind and go back to Egypt. God wanted His people to leave Egypt where they were slaves. He had a new home for them. Moses had been quiet and shy, but he became brave.

Pharaoh was stubborn. God sent ten different disasters to Egypt, and Moses warned Pharaoh when each disaster was coming. All ten disasters came to Egypt before Pharaoh allowed Moses and God's people to leave.

God took the courage of Moses, who thought he had already done the best he could, and he used that courage to save His people. Moses served God and God blessed him for it.

The Bible has tons of examples of people who served God. Let's look at some of them.

1. What was the "Promised Land" that Moses led the people toward?
  a. Babylon
  b. Syria
  c. Galatia
  d. Canaan

2. When Naaman was stricken with leprosy, the person who told him to go see the prophet Elisha was a young girl who was serving
  a. Elisha's servant
  b. Naaman's wife
  c. Queen Esther
  d. Deborah the judge and prophetess

3. When Peter was serving God by preaching the Good News about Jesus, Herod put Peter in prison. God sent _____ who freed Peter from prison.
  a. a soldier
  b. a disciple
  c. an angel
  d. a locksmith

4. Who served the church on the island of Crete—and got a book of the Bible named for him?
  a. Titus
  b. Philemon
  c. James
  d. Epaphroditus

5. When David played his soothing harp, David was serving
   a. Elisha the prophet
   b. Saul the king
   c. Moses the leader
   d. Abraham the friend of God

6. How long did Jacob serve a man named Laban in order to marry his daughter Rachel?
   a. 2 weeks
   b. 10 months
   c. 14 years
   d. a lifetime

7. When Samuel was a boy, his mother, Hannah, dedicated him to the Lord. Samuel lived in the temple and served
   a. his mother
   b. the priest, Eli
   c. the Lord
   d. b and c

☆ ANSWERS ☆

1. d (Genesis 17:8)

2. b (2 Kings 5:2-3)

3. c (Acts 12:7)

4. a (Titus 1:5)

5. b (1 Samuel 16:23)

6. c (Genesis 29:26-27. Jacob said he would work seven years for Rachel, but then was tricked into marrying her sister, Leah. So he worked another seven years for Rachel.)

7. d (1 Samuel 3:8-9)

QUIZ 42

SINCERITY

(being real and true)

God uses many things to get people's attention. For some, it might be a song that makes them think about God for the first time. For others, it may be a friend who points them to the Lord. For Charles Spurgeon, it was a verse. In Isaiah 45:22, God said, "Look to Me and be saved, all the ends of the earth. For I am God, and there is no other."

Within a year of beginning his journey with Jesus, Charles preached his first sermon. Within four years, he was a preacher with a sincere desire to tell everyone the Good News about Jesus. By the age of twenty-two, he was the most popular preacher in all of England.

God gave Charles Spurgeon a great gift. He could preach, write, and care deeply for people. But he had to remember that the message he shared was not his but God's. Charles wasn't given the job of impressing people by how well he could speak. It was to make sure he delivered the message God had in His Word.

Charles's sincerity in serving God is an example of how God wants *you* to be. Let's see what the Bible says about sincerity.

1. Jesus said that to worship God, we must worship in spirit and in _____.
   a. soul
   b. truth
   c. purity
   d. faith

2. The apostle John urged Christians to love others "by what we do and in truth," not just by what?
   a. our thoughts
   b. our talk
   c. our sympathy
   d. our giveaway junk

3. Who said about his relationship with Jesus, "He must become more important. I must become less important"?
   a. Joseph, Mary's husband
   b. the apostle John
   c. John the Baptist
   d. "Doubting" Thomas

4. Even though Judas betrayed Him, Jesus sincerely loved Judas Iscariot. When Judas brought soldiers to arrest Him, Jesus called His disciple
   a. Dude!
   b. My child
   c. Beloved
   d. Friend

5. Jesus' sincere love for His friend Lazarus was shown by His _____ when Lazarus died.
    a. anger
    b. silence
    c. tears
    d. all the above

6. Which of these women is *not* mentioned in the Bible as someone who followed Jesus and supported Him with her money?
    a. Mary Magdalene
    b. Joanna, the wife of Chuza
    c. Susanna
    d. Jezebel

7. An Italian army captain named Cornelius sincerely believed in God. Whom did God send to tell Cornelius the Good News about Jesus?
    a. Mary
    b. Philip
    c. Matthew
    d. Peter

☆ ANSWERS ☆

1. b (John 4:24)

2. b (1 John 3:18)

3. c (John 3:30)

4. d (Matthew 26:50)

5. c (John 11:35)

6. d (Luke 8:1–3)

7. d (Acts 10:30–33)

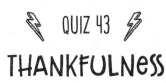

QUIZ 43

THANKFULNESS

(feeling appreciation)

Some people are so successful that it's hard to list everything they've done. Kyle Snyder is one of those people. He's an amazing wrestler who won many matches and titles in high school and college. He also did very well at the Olympics.

But something else sets Kyle apart from other wrestlers. Once during a match at a competitor's school, a school worker was doing his best to make sure each wrestler had plenty of water to drink. Kyle was the only one who thanked the man for his thoughtfulness. And he thanked the man more than once.

Kyle became a Christian in high school, and he allowed God to direct his choices. That meant that Kyle chose to work hard and show thankfulness. He knew that "you are to give thanks for what God has done for you" (Ephesians 5:4).

In life, good things will happen and bad things will happen. Be grateful that God has a plan for *everything* that happens. Thank Him even in the bad times, knowing He is going to make all things come out good.

Now, do you remember what the Bible says about thankfulness?

1. A verse in 2 Corinthians says to give thanks to God for His amazing gift to you. That gift is
   a. salvation through Jesus
   b. good health
   c. money to live on
   d. your parents

2. According to the apostle Paul, when should Christians give thanks?
   a. each morning
   b. with every meal
   c. when times are good
   d. in everything

3. In which of Jesus' miracles did He stop beforehand and offer thanks to God the Father?
   a. the raising of Lazarus from the dead
   b. the feeding of the 5,000
   c. the healing of a demon-filled man called Many (or Legion)
   d. a and b

4. In Jesus' parable about the Pharisee and the tax collector, the Pharisee bragged about himself and said that he was thankful
   a. that he was not like other men
   b. that he went without food twice a week
   c. that he gave God a certain amount of his pay
   d. all the above

5. According to the Psalms, where should we go "giving thanks"?
   a. into God's gates
   b. into all the world
   c. into the mountains
   d. into the fiery furnace

6. When the Israelites finished rebuilding the wall around Jerusalem, Nehemiah asked two large groups of _____ to lead the people in raising thanks to God.
   a. tubas
   b. singers
   c. warriors
   d. priests

7. When Jesus healed 10 men with a skin disease called leprosy, how many came back to thank Him?
   a. all 10
   b. none of them
   c. half of them
   d. only 1

☆ ANSWERS ☆

1. a (2 Corinthians 9:15)

2. d (1 Thessalonians 5:18)

3. d (John 11:1 44; Matthew 14:15-21)

4. d (Luke 18:11-12. If your prayers of thanks
   are all about how great *you* are,
   they probably aren't very good prayers.)

5. a (Psalm 100:4)

6. b (Nehemiah 12:31)

7. d (Luke 17:11-19)

🗲 QUIZ 44 🗲

TRUST

(to depend on someone or something)

Jesus had twelve disciples. One of them was Simon Peter. He loved following Jesus, but Peter was a bit of a promise breaker. Maybe you've made a promise you meant to keep but didn't. Or maybe someone made a promise to you and broke it.

Once, Peter saw Jesus walking on water and wanted to walk out to greet Him. Jesus told Peter he could, but then when Peter "saw the strong wind, he was afraid. He began to go down in the water. He cried out, 'Lord, save me!' At once Jesus put out His hand and took hold of him. Jesus said to Peter, 'You have so little faith! Why did you doubt?'" (Matthew 14:30–31).

That was Peter's style. He wanted to trust Jesus with everything, but he kept falling back into his old habits. He seemed to speak his mind and then regret it. He kept making promises he couldn't keep.

Jesus patiently taught Peter to trust Him. Peter would be used to build the church God had in mind for His family. Jesus the Master kept His promises and helped Peter the disciple keep his promises too.

Do you trust that God has a good plan for you? Do you trust even when it's hard to believe? Perhaps the questions that follow will help you build your trust in Jesus.

1. Peter's trust in God grew, and one time when Peter was in prison, God sent an angel
   a. to bring him food
   b. to help him write the book of 1 Peter
   c. to set him free
   d. all the above

2. Because Elizabeth trusted God, she gave birth to John the Baptist
   a. when she was old
   b. when she was a teenager
   c. when she had no midwife
   d. when she had no husband

3. Because two Jewish nurses, Shiphrah and Puah, trusted God, they disobeyed the pharaoh's order to kill Hebrew baby boys. How did God reward them?
   a. He protected them from Pharaoh's anger
   b. He honored them in the Bible
   c. He gave them families of their own
   d. all the above

4. Because Abraham trusted God, he believed that if he obeyed the Lord's command to sacrifice his son Isaac, God would
   a. give him another son in place of Isaac
   b. bring Isaac back from the dead
   c. immediately take Abraham to heaven with Isaac
   d. make him completely forget the experience

5. The book of Proverbs says you are to trust in the Lord
   a. with all your money
   b. when there's no one else left to trust
   c. with all your heart
   d. when things get hard

6. Which king of Judah was known for his trust in God, which meant "there was no one like him among all the kings of Judah before him or after him"?
   a. Manasseh
   b. Rehoboam
   c. Zedekiah
   d. Hezekiah

7. According to the prophet Isaiah, God will keep the person who trusts in Him in perfect
   a. health
   b. peace
   c. safety
   d. cell phone reception

☆ ANSWERS ☆

1. c (Acts 12:6–10)

2. a (Luke 1:7)

3. d (Exodus 1:15–21)

4. b (Hebrews 11:17–19)

5. c (Proverbs 3:5)

6. d (2 Kings 18:5)

7. b (Isaiah 26:3)

UNDERSTANDING

(to get the meaning of something)

Paul was a bully. But he also wrote more than a dozen books in the Bible. How did that happen? (To be fair, Paul wasn't a bully when he wrote the books. That's important to remember.)

After Jesus rose from the dead and went back to heaven, those who followed Him started churches. A lot of people became Christians. Paul (then called Saul) had been part of a group that wanted everyone to forget about Jesus. Saul picked on Christians. He thought he was important because he kept finding Christians to punish.

Then something amazing happened: Jesus appeared to Saul on the Damascus road and asked him why he was acting that way. Saul immediately knew the voice belonged to Jesus, and that he had been very wrong about Christians. Meeting Jesus changes everything.

Paul now understood that what he had been doing was wrong. And he spent the rest of his life telling people that Jesus is God's Son—that forgiveness and eternal life are gifts He offers to those who believe in Him.

You may not always understand why God does the things He does—but He understands and He wants you to trust Him. As you answer these quiz questions, look for examples to follow so you too might understand and trust God more.

1. Jesus said He spoke in picture stories (or parables) so that some people would understand and others wouldn't. What was the difference in people's ability to understand?

    a. some had much more education

    b. some were born with bigger brains

    c. some people just didn't care

    d. God shared His secrets with certain people

2. At first Mary and her sister Martha didn't understand why Jesus had let their brother Lazarus die instead of healing him. What did Jesus tell them?

    a. Lazarus was better off in heaven now

    b. Lazarus's death would allow Jesus to show God's shining-greatness (or glory)

    c. Mary and Martha needed to rely more on themselves

    d. the twelve disciples would step up to care for Mary and Martha

3. According to the Proverbs, people of understanding

    a. keep quiet

    b. win favor

    c. are slow to get angry

    d. all the above

4. Who prayed by saying, "I ask God to fill you with the wisdom and understanding the Holy Spirit gives"?

    a. Jesus

    b. Daniel

    c. Priscilla and Aquila

    d. Paul

5. Who told Egypt's pharaoh to "look for a man who is understanding and wise" to prepare the land for a time when food would be scarce?

    a. Pharaoh's baker
    b. Benjamin
    c. Pharaoh's cup-carrier
    d. Joseph

6. Because God gave Daniel knowledge and understanding, he was able to

    a. interpret dreams
    b. organize the king's banquets
    c. translate the record of Babylon into Hebrew
    d. prescribe medicine

7. According to the apostle Paul, where are all the "riches of wisdom and understanding" hidden?

    a. in the ark of the covenant
    b. in scripture
    c. in Christ
    d. in Mesopotamia

☆ ANSWERS ☆

1. d (Matthew 13:10–12)

2. b (John 11:38–40. Jesus raised Lazarus from the dead!)

3. d (Proverbs 11:12; 13:15; 14:29)

4. d (Colossians 1:9)

5. d (Genesis 41:33–40)

6. a (Daniel 5:12)

7. c (Colossians 2:3)

VIRTUE

(goodness; knowing right from wrong)

George Washington Carver was born into slavery. But he became one of the most well-known black scientists in the United States. People grew to respect him for his knowledge of plants and farming. George was also wise when it came to living life as a Christian.

As a teacher, George Washington Carver taught eight virtues to his students. He would tell them, "Be clean both inside and out. Neither look up to the rich nor down on the poor. Lose, if need be, without squealing. Win without bragging. Always be considerate of women, children, and older people. Be too brave to lie. Be too generous to cheat. Take your share of the world and let others take theirs." George made sure his wisdom matched God's Word.

The Bible teaches many other virtues in addition to the ones George Washington Carver taught. Let's find out what you know about these.

1. The Golden Rule which says, "Do for other people whatever you would like to have them do for you" can be found in which of the following books of the Bible?

  a. Genesis
  b. Psalms
  c. Matthew
  d. 2 John

2. The apostle Paul urged Christians to always think about things that are

  a. true and respected
  b. right and pure
  c. lovely and well thought of
  d. all the above

3. The apostle Paul told the people who lived in Colosse to be compassionate, kind, and forgiving, and over all of those virtues to put on _____ which holds everything together perfectly.

  a. peace
  b. love
  c. honesty
  d. faith

4. In the book of Galatians, the virtues of "love, joy, peace, not giving up, being kind, being good, having faith, being gentle, and being the boss over our own desires" are known as

  a. the virtues of Jesus
  b. the signs of discipleship
  c. the gifts of the heaven
  d. the fruit of the Spirit

5. The book of Proverbs says that a virtuous woman (or a good wife) is worth far more than
   a. gold
   b. rubies
   c. diamonds
   d. gourmet jelly beans

6. What important Bible woman heard an angel tell her, "You are honored very much. You are a favored woman. The Lord is with you. You are chosen from among many women."
   a. Miriam
   b. Deborah
   c. Mary
   d. Mary Magdalene

7. When God told the ancient Israelites that they should have "a full and fair weight," what did He mean?
   a. too much dieting was not virtuous
   b. they should be honest when they bought and sold things
   c. offerings to the temple should be heavy
   d. wrestling matches should include guys in the same weight class

☆ ANSWERS ☆

1. c (Matthew 7:12)

2. d (Philippians 4:8)

3. b (Colossians 3:12–14)

4. d (Galatians 5:22–23)

5. b (Proverbs 31:10)

6. c (Luke 1:26–28)

7. b (Deuteronomy 25:13–16)

QUIZ 47

WAITING

(being patient)

Drew Brees has been the quarterback for the New Orleans Saints football team. He has won lots of awards and has broken many records.

When Drew was young, his parents divorced. His mom didn't stay close to her kids, and as a teenager, Drew was discouraged. He wondered if he had a purpose. It seemed as if everything that could go wrong did go wrong.

That's when Drew gave his future to Jesus. He knew it was time to really follow the Lord, to wait and see what God wanted him to do. Drew would later say, "All I have to do is just give my best, commit the rest to Him. Everything else is taken care of. That takes the weight off anybody's shoulders. . .you've got somebody looking out for you."

Drew could have spent his time being jealous of people who had both parents, or of people who were close to their moms, or of people who always seemed to know what God wanted them to do with their lives. But he didn't waste time doing those things. He waited on God's direction—and his life has turned out very well.

Waiting on God to show you what He wants you to do is time well spent. Let's see what God's Word has to say about the waiting game.

1. While Hannah was waiting to see if she would ever have a child, she
    a. cried really hard
    b. prayed to God
    c. got bullied by a mean woman
    d. all the above

2. After His resurrection but before He returned to heaven, Jesus told the disciples to wait in Jerusalem for what?
    a. His second coming
    b. the prophecy of Daniel
    c. the Holy Spirit's arrival
    d. the conversion of Saul

3. What Old Testament character, who suffered terribly, is described in the New Testament as patient?
    a. Jephthah
    b. Job
    c. Jeremiah
    d. Jonah

4. The book of Psalms says we should wait _____ for the Lord to do what He says He will do.
    a. busily
    b. excitedly
    c. patiently
    d. manfully

5. The book of Lamentations says that people who wait on the Lord will find that He is

a. good
b. generous
c. powerful
d. pleased

6. Because Abraham was willing to wait for God, what did he get?

a. a Mediterranean cruise
b. flocks and herds
c. an angel visit
d. God's promise

7. According to the book of 2 Corinthians, what is one thing you should *never* wait to do?

a. be saved
b. start exercising
c. read good books
d. tell mom you love her

☆ ANSWERS ☆

1. d (1 Samuel 1:7, 10)

2. c (Acts 1:4–5)

3. b (James 5:11 KJV)

4. c (Psalm 37:7 KJV)

5. a (Lamentations 3:25. But God is all of those other things too!)

6. d (Hebrews 6:13–15)

7. a (2 Corinthians 6:2)

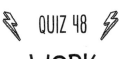

QUIZ 48

WORK

(a job to do)

God has jobs for people who preach. He has jobs for missionaries. He has jobs for people who write, play sports, and teach children. You might be surprised to know that God can use *anyone* because He has jobs for *everyone*.

Nate Saint knew how to fix airplanes. He grew up in a family that liked to dream big, fix things, and fly through the air. Nate loved Jesus but didn't think of himself as a typical missionary. Some people he worked with were translating Bibles into the languages of the people they worked with. Some shared Jesus from village to village. Nate made sure they could get there in a reliable plane.

The Bible says that those who did what God wanted when they were alive might hear God tell them they did a good job. He might say something like, "You have done well. You are a good and faithful servant" (Matthew 25:23).

God has a job for you. Do it willingly. Do it carefully. Do it faithfully.

Now let's see how good a job you do answering the quiz questions that follow!

1. After Adam ate the forbidden fruit of the tree of the knowledge of good and evil, God told him that now he would have to work hard

    a. growing his own food

    b. breaking rocks in a quarry

    c. keeping the animals from fighting

    d. picking up apples in the fall

2. The Bible says you are to do your work with all your heart. And to do it for the Lord and not for

    a. the money

    b. fame

    c. the king

    d. men

3. In Egypt Joseph first worked for Potiphar, then a jailer, and then Pharaoh. Joseph did well in whatever work he did because God

    a. was with him

    b. showed him kindness

    c. gave him favor

    d. all the above

4. While Nehemiah was helping to rebuild the walls of Jerusalem, he did his work with one hand and in his other hand he held

    a. a drink

    b. a weapon for protection

    c. a scroll of scripture

    d. a picture of his wife

5. On the seventh day of creation, God ended His work, then
a. rested
b. tested
c. jested
d. nested

6. To keep them from starving, Naomi told Ruth she should work in a nearby field
a. planting flowers
b. pulling weeds
c. picking grapes
d. gathering up leftover grain

7. What did Jesus promise to everyone whose work was heavy and tiring, if they came to Him?
a. a helper to cut the load in half
b. angels to take over
c. a cool drink of water
d. rest

☆ ANSWERS ☆

1. a (Genesis 3:17-19. The work itself wasn't a punishment—Adam had worked before. But after sin was in the world, the work was a chore, not a joy.)

2. d (Colossians 3:23-24)

3. d (Genesis 39:20-23)

4. b (Nehemiah 4:17)

5. a (Genesis 2:2-3)

6. d (Ruth 2:2)

7. d. (Matthew 11:28)

⚡ QUIZ 49 ⚡

YEARNING

(wishing hard for something)

Bart Millard wanted a father who loved him. He wanted a father who encouraged him. He wanted a father who would listen. None of those things described Bart's dad.

Bart wanted to be a football player to please his dad. While playing in high school, he broke both of his ankles. That ended any thought of making his dad happy.

But God had something new for Bart to do—*sing*. He joined his high school choir and sang in his church. This was a surprise for Bart. He didn't think he could sing.

If he was going to sing, Bart wanted to sing Christian music, but something seemed to stop him. He was still very angry with a father who didn't seem to love him. But God taught Bart, and he began to learn a lot about being a Christian. God became the good Father that Bart never had.

God loved and encouraged Bart. Because God changed him, Bart could write songs that pointed hurting people back to God.

When God gives you a yearning to do something good, He will make it happen in His own time. Now, in the following quiz, see how much you're learning about yearning!

1. Jacob's wife Rachel yearned to have a child. After a long time, God finally blessed her with a son she named

    a. Joseph
    b. Jacob Jr.
    c. Jesse
    d. John

2. Jesus knew that when He ascended to heaven, His disciples would miss Him and yearn to see Him. So the disciples were promised Jesus would

    a. one day see them in heaven
    b. come back again some day
    c. visit them in their dreams
    d. hear and answer their prayers

3. Zechariah and Elizabeth yearned to have a child, but when an angel told the old priest he would have a son, Zechariah didn't believe him. So the angel

    a. made Zechariah unable to speak until his son was born
    b. lifted Zechariah up to heaven
    c. sadly told Zechariah he had little faith
    d. blinded Zechariah with a flash of lightning

4. What did a psalm writer say his soul yearned for—that he wanted so much he became weak?

    a. to be in the Lord's house
    b. to find peace on earth
    c. to build a house of cedar
    d. to teach the world to sing

5. Haman yearned to kill Mordecai and all the Jews but instead Haman ended up
  a. having to honor Mordecai
  b. killed on the tower he built to hang Mordecai
  c. working in the king's stable
  d. a and b

6. David's son, Absalom, yearned to be king instead of his father so Absalom
  a. told the people that he cared about them more than David
  b. gathered an army to fight his father
  c. declared himself king
  d. all the above

7. What does the book of Proverbs say a fulfilled yearning (or longing or desire) is?
  a. lucky for you
  b. the first step to success
  c. sweet to the soul
  d. something to be proud of

☆ ANSWERS ☆

1. a (Genesis 30:22–24)

2. b (Acts 1:9–11)

3. a (Luke 1:19–20)

4. a (Psalm 84:2)

5. d (Esther 6:10; 7:9–10)

6. d (2 Samuel 15:4, 10; 17:1–2. These bad yearnings ended up getting Absalom killed.)

7. c (Proverbs 13:19)

ZeAL

(excitement or passion for something)

Do you like adventure? If so, you would probably get along very well with Andrew van der Bijl. Most people call him "Brother Andrew" because it's much easier to say.

Andrew trained to be a missionary and then traveled to countries that didn't want Christians to visit. Because God was leading, Andrew could say to God, "Whenever, wherever, however You want me, I'll go. . . . I'll begin this very minute. Lord, as I stand up from this place, and as I take my first step forward, will You consider this a step toward complete obedience to You?"

Andrew became known as "God's Smuggler" because he was able to sneak Bibles into countries where Bibles were hard to get. Government leaders didn't want them, yet the people needed them. Andrew would say that God did it. Andrew would be right.

Brother Andrew's story is a story of God's adventurer. He did what few other people felt brave enough to do. Andrew knew that the Bible is God's Word. He knew that if people could read it for themselves, they could meet God. He knew that if people met God, the world would change.

Brother Andrew had a zeal for God and for spreading His Word. Let's see how much zeal some people in the Bible had for God.

1. Through the prophet Haggai, God scolded the Israelites because their zeal was to _____ instead of repairing and rebuilding His temple.

    a. build houses for themselves
    b. buy and sell cattle
    c. organize sporting events
    d. mine for gold

2. When evil men plotted against Daniel, he showed his zeal for God by

    a. mocking the evil men
    b. preaching on the street corners
    c. copying scrolls of scripture by hand
    d. praying three times a day

3. What did Daniel say would happen to people who were wise and zealous to "lead many to do what is right and good"?

    a. they would have songs written about them
    b. they would make the world a happier place
    c. they would shine like the stars forever
    d. they would appear on TV

4. Even though he saw the miracle of a burning bush, Moses had no zeal to do what God called him to do. So God

    a. promised to be with Moses
    b. promised to perform mighty acts on Moses' behalf
    c. sent Aaron to help Moses
    d. all the above

5. What Old Testament prophet, who defeated 450 prophets of the false god Baal, said he had been very zealous for the Lord God?

    a. Elijah

    b. Micah

    c. Isaiah

    d. Zechariah

6. The church in Laodicea had lost its zeal, and Jesus said He didn't like the people's "lukewarm" ways. What did He threaten to do with them?

    a. light a fire under them

    b. cast them into a snowbank

    c. shine the light of the sun on their works

    d. spit them out of His mouth

7. Jesus told the people in Laodicea that His strong words were spoken in love. What did He want them to do to regain their zeal for Him?

    a. be sorry for their sins and turn from them

    b. pray without ceasing

    c. sell all they had to give to the poor

    d. memorize 200 Bible verses

☆ ANSWERS ☆

1. a (Haggai 1:2–9)

2. d (Daniel 6:10)

3. c (Daniel 12:3)

4. d (Exodus 3:12–14, 20; 4:14–17)

5. a (1 Kings 18:22)

6. d (Revelation 3:15–16)

7. a (Revelation 3:19)

MORE FOR BRAVE (AND ADVENTUROUS) BOYS!

Boys are history-makers! And this deeply
compelling storybook proves it! Just for boys
ages 8 and up, this collection of 100 adventurous stories of Christian men—from the Bible,
history, and today—will empower you to know
and understand how men of great character
have made an impact in the world and how
much smaller our faith (and the biblical
record) would be without them.

Hardback / 978-1-64352-356-9 / $16.99